HITCHED
cooking for two

*with special thanks to
Amelina Jones
for her beautifully
'in love' illustrations.*

Helen Bartlett

HITCHED
cooking for two

Copyright © Helen Bartlett 2017
Illustrations Copyright © Amelina Jones 2017

Published by Giant Mountain Publishing
www.giantmountainpublishing.com

ISBN 978-1-9997511-1-1
All rights reserved

No part of this publication may be reproduced, stored in a retrieval system, copied, or transmitted in any other form or by any means, electronic or mechanical, by photocopying, recording or otherwise, without prior written permission from the publisher.

British Library Cataloguing in Publication Data
available on request

Printed and bound in Spain by the Fullcolor Printcolor, Barcelona

HITCHED
cooking for two

Helen Bartlett

CONTENTS

INTRODUCTION 8 - 11

EVERYDAY 12 - 47

HEALTHY 48 - 61

AT HOME 62 - 97

PICNIC 98 - 127

ENTERTAINING 128 - 153

INDEX 154 - 157

STORE CUPBOARD 158

INTRODUCTION

Hitched talk

So maybe there's a commitment somewhere, it could simply be to look after *you* and to have a better balance in your life. Or perhaps you share a dog (or handbag), maybe you're settling down, sharing an apartment or actually getting married - whatever your situation this cookbook is for you with its focus on the loving, sharing nature of food. The therapy part is living beyond the ordinary world and really connecting with another soul (hand in hand, across a table) over food - it's a Doris and Rock romance all the way.

Taking time to cook is therapy for de stressing, caring and sharing - it's being creative and it brings people together. It's also a positive, energizing experience that's fully in the moment, allowing you to step off the world for a while. You know you're hooked when you look forward to cooking at the end of your day, when you start planning for the end of the week to cook up something special and when you shop early at the local market coming home, arms laden.

For this book I am in the back of a London taxi cab going home, I've told the driver (who's incidentally from the Caribbean) to go from A to B, I'm going to pay for the journey and I trust him to get me there safely. When I arrive at destination B the driver says there's nothing to pay, oh that's not possible I say handing a note his way, no he says beaming, it's just for love and (he paused) I was going your way!

The recipes are grouped into chapters starting with *everyday* - morning till night, some quick, some to come home to and some as an aid to winding down after a really hard day. Then there's *healthy* for clean dishes - full of market produce on the raw side and on to *at home* with some more time consuming recipes to make on a whim or to rustle up for a late start to the day. *Picnic* comes next, a chapter of food for when you want to graze - put your feet up, be informal, not get dressed or to take outside. The last section is *entertaining* - that's in style and with flair, for when you want or maybe need to impress.

The recipes in this book can all be prepared without special gadgetry using basic equipment (oven, hob and fridge, freezer) and tools that you would probably already have in your kitchen, such as a good set of pans in all sizes, some basic baking equipment, a good range of utensils and a standard food processor. If you have a mandolin and a conical sieve these are also handy and in the back of the book you will find a list of some of the store cupboard essentials used in the recipes.

The next couple of pages are about keeping a healthy kitchen, which you may prefer to do as naturally as possible. It's not to spoil the spontaneous enjoyment of eating and cooking or to worry you so much that you decide not to cook at all. It's there to be a 'second nature' good practice guide as opposed to an antibacterial overkill. If you're familiar with all of this then skip the next part, if you're not fully aware then read on.

Keeping a healthy kitchen

Keeping a healthy kitchen is about controlling harmful bacteria which can cause serious illness. The main points are Cross-contamination, Cleaning, Chilling and Cooking – known in the business as the 4 Cs.

Cross-contamination. Cross contamination is when bacteria are spread between food, surfaces or equipment. This is most likely to happen when raw food (meat) touches (or drips onto) ready-to-eat food, equipment or surfaces.

Cleaning. Effective cleaning gets rid of bacteria on hands, equipment and surfaces. Keeping the kitchen preparation well organized, separating tasks and equipment, tidying and cleaning as you go helps to prevent cross contamination.

Chilling. Chilling food properly helps to stop harmful bacteria from growing and by keeping the fridge in good order there is less risk of contamination. Separate food in suitable storage boxes - raw meats and fish go in the bottom, raw chicken should be completely separated – in the trade these boxes are labelled red, fish is labelled blue. The next shelf up is for clean, ready to eat, raw food such as washed salad, fruit and vegetables – these are labelled green. The top two shelves are for prepared and cooked foods including cooked meat – these are labelled yellow. Food should be well covered and dated. Dairy (and bakery) are labelled white. The temperature should be under 5 degrees C. Defrost foods in the fridge in a container and dispose of any resulting liquid. Cooked food or leftovers should not be left out of the fridge for more than 1 hour.

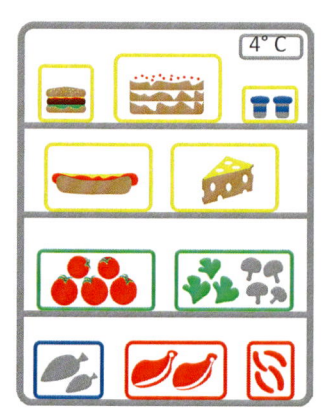

Sensible fridge layout

Cooking. Cook or reheat food thoroughly to a high temperature, making sure that it is steaming hot all the way through to a minimum of 73.9° C /165° F. Beef and lamb are examples of meat that can be eaten rare – harmful bacteria can be on the outside so sear the meat on the outside at a high temperature to kill any bacteria that might be present. For minced beef or lamb and any other meat that has been ground such as burgers and sausages, any harmful bacteria present can be spread from the outside through to the middle so these should be thoroughly cooked to 73.9° C /165° F. One test for this is to pierce the thickest part of the meat with a fork – when properly cooked the juices should run clear but if in doubt use a meat thermometer.

Raw poultry contains harmful bacteria throughout, it needs careful handling when unwrapping, prepping and cooking. (Washing raw chicken can spread bacteria too as many things could be in the splash zone near the sink). One way to effectively lower contamination risks is to wear disposable gloves and to do any raw prep work completely separately from any other, cleaning and disinfecting the work surface and every piece of equipment thoroughly before moving on. Poultry needs to be cooked right through to be safe, for a whole bird insert a knife between the inner thigh and body, pull apart slightly, insert the thermometer, the juices should run clear with no trace of pink and the safe temperature for poultry is 80° C /175° F.

The *danger zone* temperatures for food are between 4.4° C /40° F and 60° C /140° F, if food is left for two long in this zone, harmful bacteria can grow.

It is good practice to keep cold food *cold* and hot food *hot*.

To get rid of odors on boards and counter tops, lemon juice is effective.

For washing your fruit and vegetables before putting away, a solution of vinegar and water effectively removes (almost all) bacteria that could be present - use a solution of 3 parts water: 1 part vinegar. For most fruits and vegetables, it is easiest to fill a large bowl with the vinegar solution, pop in the fruits and veg (try to buy organic un waxed fruit) and scrub the surface of each one gently, then rinse in water and dry with kitchen paper. For a surface spray you can also fill a spray bottle with the solution.

For most of your day to day cleaning, scalding hot water and regular detergent or soap will do the job. As a general cleaning rule, first clean up as much as possible with absorbent **kitchen paper** and dispose of this, clean with detergent and hot water and rinse. Apply disinfectant when necessary, air dry or wipe dry with kitchen paper after a few minutes.

For cleaning after handling raw meat, you need to go a step further to disinfect. There are several ways to do this and without getting in too deep with the pros and cons, here are some of the possibilities.

There is bleach (which is toxic), use this in a dilute solution (1 teaspoon to 1000ml) to disinfect - for a wash up bowl situation and as a surface spray.

There are also more 'green' disinfectants that are relatively non-toxic.

Many natural essential oils are antibacterial such as tea tree, thyme, lemon, cinnamon, oregano, lavender and rosemary so you could make your own natural disinfectant spray (ideally in a glass bottle) using a solution of 30ml alcohol (99% pure) with 30 drops added essential oils. There are many essential oils that are also antiviral so you can also use these when travelling and as effective room sprays.

When cleaning down after handling raw meat, scrape the surface / chopping board clean with a metal scraper and **remove any traces of the raw meat from all utensils** with **disposable kitchen paper** before you take these to the sink to be washed. The sponge, brush and wiping cloth that you then use to clean and disinfect the utensils and work surfaces should also be well cleaned and disinfected.

In the trade it is a requirement to use different coloured utensils for separate tasks right down to the cleaning equipment. In the home you may decide to have two separate chopping boards, one for raw meat and one for vegetables, colour coded or not, this alone is useless unless each are properly cleaned (and dried). And, there is still nothing wrong with using a wooden chopping board properly scrubbed clean and disinfected when necessary.

EVERYDAY

Muesli bar 14 - 15

Big bowl breakfast 16 - 17

Stuffed mushrooms 18 - 19

Chorizo and potatoes 20 - 21

Asian chicken 22 - 23

Lamb tagine 24 - 26

Meatless meatballs 27 - 29

Spiced chicken 30 - 31

Canneloni 32 - 35

Moussaka 36 - 38

Stuffed aubergine 39 - 41

Vegetarian sausage 42 - 44

Ravioli 45 - 47

Muesli bar

Muesli Bar

For those with no time, this is guaranteed to get you moving, full of protein and fibre.

Utensils: mixing bowl, sharp knife, kitchen film, greaseproof paper
Equipment: food processor

50g whole almonds (with their skins on)
50g whole prunes (pitted)
50g dried apricots
50g dried cranberries
50g oats (porridge or whole)
2 tablespoon mild runny honey

Put all the ingredients into the food processor, churn well until you have a good, roughly ground texture. Add the honey.
Transfer to a mixing bowl and bring together using your hands to form a stiff lump. Place onto a sheet of greaseproof paper. Lay another sheet on top and press down with the palms of your hands to block out a rectangular shape about 1 - 1.5cm thick. Cut into small bars and wrap each individually in kitchen film so they don't dry out. Store in an air tight container.

Makes: about 10 small bars

Big Bowl Breakfast
granola, peach and coconut

Big bowl breakfast - fresh peach and coconut with granola

This is for when you need a fulfilling breakfast to give you plenty of energy. The recipe makes plenty of granola, which you can store for other days.

Utensils: large mixing bowl, large spoon, greaseproof paper
Equipment: oven, food processor

For the granola	For the breakfast bowl
180g raw organic oats	*1 nectarine*
50g walnuts	*1 peach*
50g hazelnuts	*4 tablespoons organic raw oats*
50g almonds (skins on)	*2 tablespoons organic dried coconut*
2 tablespoons runny honey	*10 tablespoons coconut milk*
2 tablespoons coconut oil	*2 tablespoons granola*

Pre-heat the oven to 180 degrees C. Line the oven tray with greaseproof paper.
Put the nuts into the processor and grind to rough crumbs, tip out into a large mixing bowl. Put the oats into the processor and grind to rough crumbs, add to the nuts. Add the honey and the oil, use your fingers to rub into the crumbs, (do very thoroughly making sure there are no dry areas – you should have a coated crumbly mixture).
Tip out onto the tray, spread out and press down a little.
Bake in a hot oven for about 12 minutes. Keep an eye on them - you are looking for an even, lightly toasted result, no burnt edges or uncooked centre. Half way through cooking move the crumbly mixture around a little with a spoon, drawing in the browner edges to the centre, and the uncooked centre outwards. When ready the crumbs should be lightly golden (toasted) all over.
Remove from the oven and leave to cool. Store in an airtight container.

For the breakfast bowl, put the oats and coconut into your bowl and soak with the milk for 10 minutes. Peel the fruit, remove the stones and finely dice - add on top of the oats. Sprinkle with granola.
Eat immediately.

Makes: breakfast bowl for 1 plus extra granola

Stuffed mushrooms

Stuffed Mushrooms

These are great for lunch or a light supper, best to do more than you think!

Utensils: chopping board and knife, frying pan, spatula,
Equipment: hob, food processor

2 slices of white bread – ground into fine bread crumbs with 1 tablespoon white flour
1 small stick of celery
1 large clove of garlic
1 tablespoon finely chopped parsley
4 large mushrooms for stuffing – the open field variety works best, with their stalks removed
3 medium sized mushrooms
1 small onion
1 small tomato
2 - 3 tablespoons extra virgin olive oil
30g butter
Salt and pepper

Gently fry the large mushrooms whole in 1 tablespoon olive oil, fry on both sides until golden and just cooked (time for this will depend on the thickness and size - button mushrooms take longer than open field mushrooms). When done, set aside.
Finely dice the tomatoes and retain their juices.
Finely chop the onion, garlic, celery and the rest of the mushrooms, sauté in 1 tablespoon of olive oil and the butter. Cook for about 2 minutes, stirring constantly.
Add the chopped parsley and breadcrumbs and continue to cook for another minute.
Add in the chopped tomatoes, stir and season well, take off the heat.
Arrange the large mushrooms in a serving dish and divide the breadcrumb mixture between them and mound it up. The mixture may look too much but pile it up high into little mountains. Serve immediately.

Makes: 2 - 4 portions

Cooking note: you could also pop the mushrooms under the grill for five minutes with or without some grated cheese to lightly golden the tops.

Chorizo and potatoes

Chorizo, new potatoes, rocket and peppers

A tasty combination of flavours and textures makes this a great supper – make sure you find a top quality fresh chorizo 'extra' if possible – this type has more piquancy than the normal.

Utensils: chopping board and knife, prep bowls, pan, small frying pan, spatula
Equipment: hob

200g new potatoes
200g fresh chorizo sausage
80g red pepper
50g rocket
30g white sweet onion
1 tablespoon fresh thyme leaves
1 clove of garlic
2 - 4 tablespoons extra virgin olive oil
Pinch of sea salt flakes

Boil the potatoes in a generous amount of boiling water for about 5-7 minutes until just done. Drain, cut in half and set aside.
Trim and de-seed the pepper. Finely slice the flesh.
Carefully remove and discard the skin from the chorizo. Dice or slice the sausage with a very sharp knife.
Peel and very finely slice the onion. Peel and very finely chop the garlic.
In a large pan sauté the cooked potato halves until lightly golden. Tip out into the serving dish(es).
Sauté the pepper strips in a little more oil, cook gently on a medium heat until soft, for about 3-5 minutes. Add to the potatoes.
Sauté the chorizo and garlic in a little more oil on a low heat. Turn the slices over and cook for about a minute on each side - just enough to warm through. Add to the potatoes and peppers.
Arrange the finely sliced onion, thyme and rocket over the potatoes.
Drizzle with olive oil and season well with salt flakes. Serve immediately.

Makes: 2- 4 portions

Asian chicken
with cashew nuts

Asian chicken with cashew nuts

A classic oriental dish without ordering takeout!

Utensils: Chopping board and knife, grater, bowls, frying pan or wok, spatula
Equipment: hob

2 medium sized chicken breasts
1 tablespoon cornflour
2 large spring onions
20g fresh ginger
2 large garlic cloves, finely grated
100g cashew nuts (unsalted)
3 tablespoons light sesame oil
1 tablespoon soy sauce
1 tablespoon sugar syrup
1 teaspoon fish sauce or oyster sauce (optional)
2 tablespoons water

Trim and finely slice the spring onions diagonally.
Peel and finely grate the ginger and the garlic.
Cut the chicken up in to small strips approximately 2cm x 1cm, dust each piece with cornflour, set aside in a bowl.
In a bowl, combine the soy, sugar syrup, ginger, garlic and water (and fish sauce if you have it).
Heat the sesame oil in a large pan or wok if you have one, stir fry the chicken pieces moving quickly on high heat to seal - for about 4 minutes.
Add the cashew nuts and spring onions, stir fry for 30 seconds, turn down the heat, add the marinade and simmer for 1 minute. Remove from the heat and it's ready to serve.

This dish goes well with fragrant basmati rice. To cook a generous portion for two persons use 250g rice. Tip into 1 litre of rapidly boiling water and boil for 5 minutes. Drain thoroughly and serve hot.

Makes: 2 portions

Cooking note: for an authentic flavour, it is important to use sesame oil, nothing else quite matches, you could also stir in pre cooked noodles into the finished dish.

Lamb tagine with cinnamon

Lamb tagine with cinnamon cooked on the hob

This fragrant North African dish can be prepared in advance and reheated gently for an instant supper.

Utensils: chopping board and knife, prep bowls, grater, large heavy bottomed pan with lid
Equipment: hob

300g lean tender lamb (leg or chump)
Salt and freshly ground pepper

250g tomatoes
160g aubergine
100g red onion
80g apple
80g Medjoul dates
50g sultanas
40g fresh ginger root
20g pine kernels
1 orange
1 generous bunch fresh coriander (roughly chopped)
1 cinnamon stick (split in two)
1 tablespoon ground cinnamon
2 teaspoons pimenton
1 teaspoon ground cumin
3 tablespoons extra virgin olive oil
1 teaspoon white sesame seeds (to garnish)

Cut the lamb into 2cm cubes, put in a large bowl and season well with salt and pepper. Add the ground cinnamon, pimenton and cumin, rub all over the meat and set aside.
Trim and finely dice the tomatoes.
Trim the aubergine, remove the skin and dice (1.5 cm cubes).
Peel and finely chop the onion. Peel the apple, remove core and finely dice.
Remove the stone from the dates, trim the top and finely slice.
Peel the ginger and finely grate. Finely zest the orange using the grater, then juice.
Heat the oil in a large heavy bottomed pan, add the cubed meat and sear each side on high heat for 30 seconds. Add the aubergines, onions and apple, continuously stir over medium heat for 2 minutes.

Add 100ml water and stir in the rest of the ingredients (except the fresh coriander and sesame seeds), turn the heat down, cover and gently cook for 15 minutes.
Add the fresh coriander and transfer to the serving dish.
Sprinkle with sesame seeds and serve. This dish goes well with steamed couscous or plain long grain rice.

Makes: 2 generous portions

Cooking note: if preparing in advance and reheating, reserve some fresh coriander to stir into the dish just before serving. Medjoul dates are the king of dates, very large and sweet but expensive so don't worry if you can't get these, the normal ones will also do.

Fragrant orange couscous salad

A quick couscous salad with no cooking involved. It goes well with stewed dishes such as tagine or you can add it to a bowl of fresh leaves and dress with vinaigrette.

Utensils: chopping board and knife, grater, large mixing bowl

250g easy cook couscous
200ml water
50g mild white onion (Spanish variety)
50g green pepper
1 small orange
1 small bunch coriander
Freshly ground black pepper
Pinch sea salt flakes

Put the couscous in a large bowl and cover with water. Leave to sit for 20 minutes.
Peel and very finely dice the onion. Trim the pepper, remove the seeds and finely dice. Finely chop the coriander. Zest the orange.
Use your finger tips or a fork to fluff up the couscous, separating all the grains (they should be light and dry).
Season sparingly, add in the prepared ingredients, mix thoroughly.
Serve at room temperature with a stewed dish such as tagine.

Makes: 2 portions

Cooking note: to serve the couscous hot, put in a bowl, cover with kitchen film and steam in the microwave for about 30 seconds.

Meatless meatballs
with tomato sauce

'Meat-less' bean balls with tomato sauce

A really tasty alternative without meat that you could even serve to a dedicated carnivore.

Utensils: Chopping board and knife, conical sieve, large pan, small pan, large bowl, spatula,
Equipment: Hob, food processor

For the balls
150g aduki beans
30g red onion
1 small stick celery
1 large clove garlic
40g dried cranberries
1 teaspoon cumin seeds
1 teaspoon dried oregano
1 teaspoon pimenton dulce (sweet)
1 tablespoon extra-virgin olive oil
1 tablespoon lime juice
Sea salt
Freshly milled black pepper
1 teaspoon white sesame seeds
1 lime

Pre-cook the beans in a large pan of boiling water for about 40 minutes – test (they need to be just cooked with plenty of bite).
Peel and finely chop the onion and garlic. Finely chop the celery.
Sauté the onion, garlic and celery gently in olive oil for 3 minutes, remove from the heat, set aside.
Finely chop the cranberries in with the oregano, cumin seeds and pimenton.
In a processor grind the cooked beans to form a rough paste, turn out into a large bowl, add the cranberry mix, the cooked onion mix and the lime juice. Mix thoroughly, season well with salt and pepper.
Use your hands to form 10 - 12 balls.

For the tomato sauce
300g tomatoes
60g onion
1 large clove garlic
1 tablespoon lime juice
1/2 teaspoon cumin seeds
1 teaspoon dried oregano
1 teaspoon pimenton dulce
10g fresh coriander
100ml tomato juice
1 tablespoon extra-virgin olive oil

Peel and finely dice the onion and garlic, sauté in olive oil in a medium-sized pan on low heat for 3 minutes.
Finely chop the tomatoes, add to the pan and continue cooking.
Add the oregano, cumin, pimenton, lime and tomato juice, simmer gently for about 3 minutes.
Remove from heat, finely chop the coriander and stir into the sauce.

To serve, gently sauté the balls in a little olive oil, add the tomato sauce, cover and gently warm through, sprinkle with sesame seeds.

Makes: 2 – 4 portions

See page 27 for image

Spiced chicken with tamarind glaze

Spiced chicken with tamarind glaze

Piquant, fiery and goes great with simple grains and / or a fresh leaf salad on the side.

Utensils: Chopping board and knife, small pan and spoon, large frying pan, prep bowls, foil or lid to cover pan
Equipment: Hob

For the tamarind glaze
60g tamarind paste (seedless)
1 teaspoon cumin seeds,
1 teaspoon pimento dulce (sweet)
1 teaspoon ground chili
2 tablespoons lime juice
1 tablespoon sesame oil
Sea salt

2 tablespoons white sesame seeds

For the chicken
2 chicken legs, each cut in half
1 tablespoon pimento dulce
1 dessertspoon corn flour
Salt and freshly ground pepper
2 tablespoons extra-virgin olive oil

200g tomatoes
1 dessertspoon cumin seeds

Combine the tamarind paste and lime juice in a small pan and gently heat until the paste softens. Add the sesame oil, cumin seeds, pimenton and chili, remove from the heat, set aside.

Season the frying pan with a little oil, add the sesame seeds and cover (they jump and pop). Shake the pan, remove from the heat when the seeds are golden, set aside.

Cut the chicken legs in half at the joints, season well and dust with the pimenton and corn flour.
Trim and finely chop the tomatoes.
Heat 2 tablespoons olive in a large frying pan, sauté the chicken pieces for 4 minutes each side to sear.
Turn down the heat, baste all over with the tamarind paste, add the chopped tomatoes and cumin seeds, cover and steam on low heat for 10 minutes.

Scatter the sesame seeds generously over the glazed chicken and serve hot or cold with steamed couscous.

Makes: 2 portions

Canneloni

Cannelloni stuffed with spinach and mushrooms

This dish takes a long time to prepare with four separate stages but is well worth the effort. It can be prepared hours (or a day) in advance and finished in the oven before serving - you can then really enjoy eating it!

Utensils: large bowl, whisk, jug, medium-sized frying pan, medium-sized saucepan, oven proof serving dish approximately 22cm x 22cm x 5cm deep, flat spatula, large plate, prep bowls
Equipment: hob, oven, food processor (optional).

For the pancakes:
80g plain white flour
2 large eggs
200ml milk
Oil for frying

To make the pancakes:
In a large bowl whisk together the flour, eggs and milk to form a smooth runny batter, pour into a jug.
Heat a little oil in the frying pan, (wipe the base with kitchen paper so you have a very thin even layer), make sure it's hot, then pour in a small amount of batter, turn the pan so that the batter covers the base, cook on high heat for 30 seconds. Using the spatula turn over and cook on the other side for 30 seconds, transfer to a plate.
If the pan looks dry, add a little more oil, if not you can continue to make more pancakes, you should have 5-6 pancakes, set aside.

For the filling:
120g fresh spinach
400g mushrooms
100g white onion
2 cloves garlic
1 tablespoon extra-virgin olive oil
40g butter unsalted
Salt and freshly ground black pepper

To make the filling:
Remove any large stalks from the spinach, discard and roughly chop the leaves.
Clean the mushrooms and finely chop.
Peel and finely dice the onion and the garlic.
In the frying pan melt the butter in the oil on medium heat, add the mushrooms, onions and garlic, sauté for 3 minutes, add the spinach, continue to sauté for 1 minute. Remove from the heat, season well, set the mix aside.

For the tomato sauce:
250g tomatoes
80g white onion
1 clove garlic
1 teaspoon dried oregano
100ml tomato juice
1 tablespoon extra-virgin olive oil
Sea salt and freshly ground black pepper

To make the tomato sauce:
Trim the tomatoes and finely chop.
Peel and finely chop the onions and garlic.
In a medium sized saucepan, heat the oil and sauté the onions and garlic on low heat for 2 minutes to soften.
Add the tomatoes, oregano and juice, simmer for 5 minutes. Remove from the heat, set aside.

For the cheese sauce:
200ml milk
40g unsalted butter
1 tablespoon plain white flour
1 bay leaf
60g parmesan cheese

If you are serving immediately, pre-heat the oven to 220 degrees C.

To make the cheese sauce:
Warm the milk and bay leaf in a small pan on low heat, leave to infuse for 10 minutes. Put the butter in a medium sized pan and melt over low heat, add the flour and beat with a spatula to form a smooth paste. Whisk in the warmed milk, continue to gently cook until the mixture has thickened, continue to whisk until thick and smooth. Stir in most of the grated cheese, set a little aside for the top of the finished dish.

To construct the dish.
Spoon half the tomato sauce into the bottom of the serving dish, spread out evenly.
Lay the pancakes out on the work surface and distribute the filling - place a sausage-shaped amount in the centre of each one.
Roll each one up and place on top of the tomato (fold side down). Pack in closely.
Spoon the rest of the tomato mix on top.
Finish by spooning over the cheese sauce to fill the entire dish.
Sprinkle the remaining grated parmesan on top.
To serve immediately, place on a foil-lined oven tray (as it may bubble over) and bake in a hot oven for 15 minutes.
Serve with a crisp green salad and a bottle of Amarone.

Makes: 4 – 6 portions

Cooking notes: if you are setting the prepared dish aside, cover tightly with cling film and refrigerate. When it comes to serving, take out of the refrigerator 2 hours in advance to bring to room temperature, pre-heat the oven to 180 degrees C and bake, middle-low shelf for 30 – 40 minutes until heated through, cover the top if necessary with foil if it starts to brown too much before the time is up.

Moussaka

Moussaka

Although commonly known as a Greek dish, this is a favourite throughout the Middle East. It's one to prepare hours or a day in advance, perhaps to make at the weekend and to enjoy early in the week. The recipe is in three parts, make each separately then put all together at the end.

Utensils: Medium-sized pan, frying pan, spatula, grater, oven proof dish (about 20 x 30cm x 6cm high)
Equipment: oven, hob

Pre-heat the oven to 220 degrees C (only if you are eating it straight after the preparation).

Part 1 – meat sauce
300g lean minced lamb
100g onion
100g tomato
100ml tomato juice
2 large cloves garlic
1 teaspoon dried oregano
1 teaspoon ground cinnamon
1 bay leaf
Sea salt and freshly ground black pepper
2 tablespoons extra virgin olive oil

Peel and finely slice the onion and garlic.
Trim and finely dice the tomato.
Sauté the onions and garlic in olive oil for 2 minutes.
Add the minced lamb, cook for another 2 minutes until lightly golden, make sure the meat does not clump, season well with salt and pepper.
Add the diced tomato, tomato juice, oregano, cinnamon and bay leaf, gently simmer for 5 minutes until reduced.

Part 2 – cook the aubergine
300g aubergine (1 medium-sized)
Extra virgin olive oil for frying

Trim the aubergine and slice approximately 0.5cm thick, sprinkle with a little salt both sides and spread out on kitchen paper for 15 minutes.
After 15 minutes, dab dry all over (they will be a little damp). Sauté the slices on high heat, in a little oil until lightly golden on each side. Drain on a kitchen paper, set aside.

Part 3 - the white sauce
300ml thick Greek yoghurt
100g hard cheese
2 egg yolks
1/2 nutmeg grated (1 teaspoon)
Freshly ground black pepper

In a large bowl, combine the yoghurt and egg yolks, whisk together until smooth. Finely grate the cheese, add the nutmeg and season generously with black pepper.

To assemble the moussaka, place a layer of fried aubergines on the base of your dish, then spread a layer of meat. Repeat the aubergine and meat layers - top with the yoghurt mixture. Bake in the hot oven, middle shelf for 20 minutes until golden. Serve with a green salad and fresh bread.

Makes: 2 - 4 portions

Cooking note: If you are making this in advance then bake in a pre-heated oven 180 degrees C for 40 minutes so that it gets hot in the middle – test with a thermometer if you wish.

Stuffed aubergine

Stuffed aubergine with spinach, lentils and sweet potato

The textured, earthy qualities of lentils pair well with the creamy aubergine, pungent garlic and fragrant coriander.

Utensils: Chopping board and knife, large bowl, conical sieve, greaseproof paper, kitchen foil, small and medium-sized pans
Equipment: oven, hob

1 large aubergine (approximately 350g)
1 sweet potato (approximately 200g)
100g puy lentils
50g fresh spinach leaves
1 small red onion
2 sticks celery
4 cloves garlic
50g sultanas (soaked in warm water)
20g fresh coriander
1 teaspoon dried oregano
Extra virgin olive oil
Sea salt
Freshly milled black pepper

Pre-heat the oven to 240 degrees C.
Prick the sweet potato all over with a fork and bake, middle shelf, hot oven for 30 minutes (test with a knife – it should be soft all the way through).

Cut the aubergine in half length-ways, drizzle generously with olive oil, wrap in greaseproof paper and then in foil, bake in a hot oven, middle shelf for 15 - 20 minutes. When cooked, remove from the oven, take out of the wrapping and set aside.

Cook the lentils in a generous amount of boiling water for about 20 minutes until just cooked, strain and set aside in a large bowl.

Peel and finely dice the onion and garlic. Finely chop the celery.
Gently sauté in 2 tablespoons olive oil for 2 minutes.
Stir in the spinach leaves and oregano, cook for 1 more minute, add to the cooked lentils.

Scoop out the aubergine flesh, cut into small pieces and fold into the mix.
Cut the sweet potato in half, scoop out the flesh, cut into pieces and fold into the mix. (you can set the skin aside to eat separately).

Drain the sultanas, add to the mix. Finely chop the coriander and add to the mix, combine thoroughly, season generously to taste.
Pile the filling back into the aubergine skins.
Serve at room temperature or put back into the hot oven for 5 minutes.

Makes: 2 large portions

Cooking note: sweet potatoes cook best without being covered

See page 39 for image

Vinaigrette

This vinaigrette is useful to have prepared in your store cupboard. As well as a dressing for salad it can be used to moisten and spice up dishes, particularly the ones that include lentils or beans.

Utensils: Chopping board and knife, bowl, whisk, grater

4 tablespoons extra virgin olive oil
1 tablespoon lemon juice
1 tablespoon apple cider vinegar
1 tablespoon sugar syrup
1 tablespoon mustard
10g fresh ginger root
1 large clove garlic
Freshly ground black pepper

Peel and finely grate the ginger and the garlic. Combine all the ingredients in a bowl and whisk until blended. Season to taste.

Cooking note: You can add in a handful of finely chopped herbs such as chives, parsley and tarragon to make a herb dressing.

Vegetarian sausages

Vegetarian sausages

Another recipe to aid winding down, get organized and really enjoy the prep.

Utensils: chopping board and knife, large pan, conical sieve, spatula, large bowl
Equipment: hob, food processor

200g mung beans
50g lentils (any small brown variety)
200g closed cap mushrooms
250g onions
6 cloves garlic
50g dried apricots
60g bread (white or brown)
30g polenta
12 fresh sage leaves
1 teaspoon thyme (fresh or dried)
3 tablespoons dried oregano
1 generous teaspoon sea salt
2 pinches freshly milled black pepper
150ml extra virgin olive oil, plus extra for frying

Put a large pan of water on to boil, add the mung beans and lentils, simmer for about 30 minutes, strain and tip out into a large mixing bowl (the lentils should be cooked soft, the mung beans cooked but with bite and texture). Grind up half the mixture in the food processor and then add the ground mixture back into the bowl.

Roughly chop the apricots and bread. Put in the food processor with the herbs, salt and pepper, churn until the mix is a fine bread-crumb texture, then add to the lentil and bean mix.

Roughly chop the mushrooms and sauté with the onions and garlic in a large pan with 2 tablespoons olive oil for 3-4 minutes. Remove from heat, transfer to the processor and finely chop (should be a near paste) then add to the lentil and bean mix.

Thoroughly mix all the ingredients together, using your hands compact the mix, it should stick together when a ball is formed. Taste and add extra seasoning if needed. Take a handful at a time and shape into sausages, you can make them as big or as small as you like, refrigerate before frying for at least 30 minutes.

When ready to eat, shallow fry the sausages in hot oil on a medium heat until very golden each side (turn carefully with a flat spatula to avoid breaking). Serve on own or with tomato salsa and green salad.

Makes: about 8 sausages depending on size

Cooking note: If you want to make large sausages, add 1 egg yolk to the mix just before forming the sausages - this will help them to hold together during the final sauté.

Vegetable crisps

These delicate crisps are a nice alternative to the shop bought ones, they can be deep fried or baked in the oven. If you want to make straight potato crisps, these are better deep fried.

Vegetables such as carrots, sweet potato, parsnip and beetroot work well in the oven. Extra virgin olive oil and seasonings to your liking such as sea salt, chilli spice and dried herbs.

To bake: pre heat the oven to 180 degrees C, line the oven tray with baking parchment. Peel the vegetables and thinly slice in large slices as they will shrink considerably - use a mandolin if you have one or a potato peeler. Lay the slices between two layers of kitchen paper to dry. Drizzle the slices all over with oil and lay out on the oven tray. Bake middle shelf for about 15 minutes until golden - the time will depend on your oven and the the thickness of slices, so keep an eye on them. Remove from the oven and season.

To deep fry, dry the slices and drop in small quantities into hot oil until lightly golden and crisp. Transfer to kitchen paper and season.

Ravioli
with serrano ham

Ravioli with serrano ham, Manchego and garlic

It's not every day you'd have time for this but if home early from a stressful, work laden day, this could be your remedy – phone off, hands on, mind drifting and a glass of full bodied red by your side.

Utensils: chopping board and knife, large bowl, rolling pin, fine sieve, large sauce pan, small sauce pan, spoon, colander, round pastry cutter about 6cm diameter, grater, wire scoop, clean damp tea towel
Equipment: hob

For the pasta
*190g plain white flour
2 large whole eggs and 1 large egg yolk
1 teaspoon extra virgin olive oil*

*Extra virgin olive oil
Sea salt
Freshly ground black pepper*

For the filling
*2 tablespoons extra virgin olive oil
2 large cloves garlic
10g unsalted butter
130g serrano ham (sliced or in one piece)
60g mild white onion
80g Manchego cheese (finely grated)*

Basil leaves for garnish

Use a sieve to finely dust the work surface with a little flour – don't over flour.
Put the flour into a large bowl, make a well in the centre, add the eggs and olive oil. Combine thoroughly, starting with a spoon and finishing with your hands and then turn out the dough onto the work surface. Knead for a couple of minutes until a soft elastic dough has formed. Press out the dough to form a large flat disc, take the rolling pin and roll away from you, turn the dough and roll again. Dust lightly with flour if need be, continue to roll, turning and working the rolling pin back and forth from alternate sides until you have a large flat shape approximately 50 x 50cm and 1mm thick.

Put a large pan of water on high heat, bring to the boil. Add a pinch of salt and a teaspoon of olive oil.

Cut out round disks with the pastry cutter, a 6cm round cutter works well but the size is up to you, cover the pasta rounds with a lightly damp tea towel whilst you work on the filling.

Peel and finely chop the onion and garlic.
Very finely chop or mince the serrano ham, set aside a small amount for garnish.
Cook all together gently in the olive oil and butter in a small pan for 3 minutes. Remove from the heat, season with black pepper and add in 50g of the cheese.
Place a spoonful of the mixture in the centre of half of the pasta disks. Use the spare egg white to moisten the edges of the disks surrounding the filling. Cover the fillings with the remaining disks, pressing firmly down with your fingers at the edges to 'pinch' each one closed.
Drop them carefully into the boiling water, cook for 3 minutes, scoop out, drain thoroughly and place on serving plate, drizzle generously with olive oil, sprinkle with the remaining cheese, fresh basil leaves and extra serrano.
Serve immediately.

Makes: 2 portions

Cooking note: any hard cheese can replace the Manchego

See page 45 for image

HEALTHY

Greek salad 12 - 14

Hawaiian salad 12 - 14

Salad of figs and avocado 12 - 14

Bacon and coriander salad 12 - 14

Langoustine, chicory & orange 12 - 14

Andalucian salad 12 - 14

Greek salad

Greek Salad

A classic combination of soft salty feta, pungent crisp peppers and leafy textures.

Utensils: chopping board and knife, large mixing bowl

50g feta cheese
60g black olives (pitted)
60g red pepper
40g rocket leaves
40g lambs lettuce
50g mild white onion
1 large garlic cloves
1 teaspoon dried oregano
1 teaspoon fresh thyme leaves
Squeeze of fresh lemon juice
Freshly ground pepper
50ml extra virgin olive oil

Cut the feta up into small cubes (about 0.5cm). Sprinkle with dried oregano and fresh thyme, season with pepper. Put into a large mixing bowl.
Trim the pepper, remove the seeds and very thinly slice the flesh.
Cut the black olives in half.
Peel and very finely slice the onion.
Peel and very finely chop the garlic.
Put all the prepared ingredients into the bowl with the feta, toss gently. Add the rocket leaves and lambs lettuce, drizzle with oil, lemon juice and season with pepper. Serve immediately.

Makes: 2 portions

Hawaiian salad

Hawaiian Salad

Sweet tropical flavours contrasting zesty lime, spring onion and chilli heat.

Utensils: chopping board and knife, prep bowls

200g fresh pineapple (flesh only, prepared weight)
200g fresh pawpaw (flesh only, prepared weight)
200g fresh melon (flesh only, prepared weight)
100g green topped spring onion
50g sweetcorn (tinned and drained)
2 green chicory heads
2 large mild yellow chillies
2 teaspoons sugar syrup*
2 large limes
Extra virgin olive oil or coconut oil if you have it
Freshly ground pepper

Cut the fruit into neat 1cm cubes, set aside in a bowl.
Trim and de-seed the chillies, finely slice.
Trim the spring onion and finely slice diagonally in long lengths.
Zest the limes (just the barest top surface for 'zestiness') then juice.
In a small bowl combine the oil, lime zest and juice and season with pepper.
Add in the chilli strips and sugar syrup.
Line the serving dish(es) with chicory leaves, add the fruit and sweetcorn then scatter over the spring onions. Pour over the dressing and serve immediately.

Makes: 2 – 4 portions

Cooking note: * If you don't have this in your larder, combine 100g caster sugar with 100ml water and simmer gently until the sugar has melted and a light syrup has formed. Cool and bottle, keeps well. In the front of the image the salad is served in banana leaves.

Salad of figs & avocado
with basil & mozzarella

Salad of figs and avocado with basil and mozzarella

When in season this is a heavenly combination – all the produce needs to be ultra-fresh and perfectly ripe.

Utensils: chopping board and knife, small pan, spoon, sieve
Equipment: hob

8 fresh purple figs
250g mozzarella (buffalo)
80g white sweet mild onion
30g fresh basil leaves
50ml extra virgin olive oil
50g raspberries
2 tablespoons caster sugar
1 tablespoons fig vinegar (or apple cider vinegar)
Extra virgin olive oil for drizzling
Freshly ground black pepper

To make the dressing
Combine raspberries, vinegar and sugar in a small pan, cook on low heat until the sugar has dissolved and a light syrup has formed. Strain through a sieve and set aside.

To construct the salad
Trim and slice the figs, lay out on the serving plate(s).
Slice the mozzarella and put next to the figs.
Peel and ultra-finely slice the onion and distribute over the top.
Slice the basil leaves and scatter over.
Drizzle the raspberry dressing over the figs.
Drizzle the whole salad with olive oil and season well with black pepper.
Serve immediately.

Makes: 2 portions

Bacon salad

Bacon and coriander salad

A great light supper with a chilled glass of white.

Utensils: chopping board and knife, frying pan and spatula, large bowl
Equipment: hob

70g lambs lettuce (or a mix of baby spinach, rocket)
½ small cucumber
1 spring onion
4 rashers lean bacon
1 tablespoon pine kernels
1 generous handful of fresh coriander leaves
½ lemon
1 teaspoon balsamic vinegar
Extra virgin olive oil
Sea salt flakes and freshly ground black pepper

Peel the cucumber, discard the skin, finely dice the flesh and season well with pepper.
Trim the spring onion, finely slice in long diagonal strips.
Cut the bacon into thin strips, sauté in a little olive oil until lightly golden, remove and set aside.
Fry the pine nuts in the bacon oil for 30 seconds until lightly golden.
In a large bowl, toss all the ingredients together, drizzle generously with olive oil, lemon juice and balsamic vinegar. Season lightly and serve immediately.

Makes: 2 portions

Langoustine, chicory and orange salad

Langoustine, chicory and orange salad

Easily a dinner party starter or a special late night supper – it needs to be prepared and eaten at once but is relatively quick to do.

Utensils: chopping board and knife, grater, small pan, spoon, prep bowls
Equipment: hob

For the salad
2 heads green chicory
8 - 12 large cooked langoustine (king prawns)
1 tender celery stick
1 scallion
2 sweet oranges
Sprigs fresh dill or fennel

For the dressing
2 tablespoons extra virgin olive oil
1 tablespoon lemon juice
20g fresh ginger root
1 tablespoon caster sugar
1 large sweet orange
Freshly ground black pepper

For the dressing
Peel and finely grate the ginger.
Finely grate the orange zest, set aside, juice the orange.
Put the orange juice and sugar into a small pan and cook over low heat a light syrup has formed.
Combine the olive oil, lemon juice and orange syrup.
Add the grated ginger and orange zest, season with black pepper.

Peel the prawns and remove the waste vein running along the arched back – make a small slit along the length of the back and pull out the vein – it can be black if full of waste or pink if not.
Cut the celery into fine sticks. Finely slice the scallions diagonally.
Cut the skin off the oranges and remove the segments with a sharp knife
Remove the outer leaves from the chicory, trim the base and arrange the leaves (fanning out from the centre) in two small bowls.
Arrange the prepared langoustines, celery, scallions and orange segments on top.
Pour the dressing over and garnish with fresh sprigs of dill or fennel.
Serve immediately.

Makes: 2 portions (starter-sized)

Andalucian salad

Andalucian Salad

For when you crave salad but not just leaves - big, colourful, sunny and a meal in itself, served practically everywhere in the region.

Utensils: chopping board and knife, prep bowls, large mixing bowl, large pan, colander, slotted spoon
Equipment: hob

200g potatoes
150g carrots
150g beetroot (pre-cooked)
150g tomatoes
50g sweet corn (drained if using tinned)
50g white onion
50g spring onion
2 little gem lettuces
2 large eggs
10g parsley
50ml extra virgin olive oil
30ml apple cider vinegar
Sea salt and freshly ground pepper

Peel and dice the potatoes, boil in a generous amount of water until tender. Add the eggs in to the boiling water as well until they are hard boiled (about 10 minutes). Drain both and set aside, season the potatoes and drizzle with olive oil.
Peel and finely slice the carrots. Trim the beetroot and slice. Trim the tomatoes and cut into segments. Trim the spring onion and finely slice.
Peel and finely slice the white onion. Finely chop the parsley.
Peel the hard boiled eggs, cut in half and season.
Combine the olive oil and vinegar in a small bowl, season with salt and pepper.
Line the serving dish(es) with the lettuce leaves.
Toss all the other ingredients gently together, (except the eggs) in a large mixing bowl. Turn out onto the lettuce leaves and dress with the vinaigrette. Place the boiled eggs on top, season and serve immediately.

Makes: 2 large salads

AT HOME

Eggs Benedict 64 - 65

Blinis with asparagus 66 - 67

Quiche 68 - 69

French onion soup 70 - 71

Simple pan fried fish 72 - 73

Spare ribs & spring rolls 74 - 77

Bakewell tart 78 - 79

Apple and almond strudel 80 - 83

Mexican chocolate tart 84 - 85

Bread 86 - 87

Scones for tea 88 - 89

Orange and almond cakes 90 - 91

Butter shorbread 92 - 93

Walnut and coffee cake 94 - 95

Ice creams 96 - 97

Eggs Benedict

Eggs Benedict

Pan-cooked bun, ham, fried eggs and Hollandaise sauce – it's all about the pleasure of cooking and making an effort, enjoying time and lingering good. Serve with coffee and be organized as it all needs to be hot.

Utensils: mixing bowl, large pan with lid, small pan and whisk
Equipment: hob

For the buns
200g white flour
2 teaspoons easy action yeast
1 teaspoon white caster sugar
1 teaspoon salt
1 tablespoon extra-virgin olive oil
100ml warm water
Extra flour for dusting
Oil for frying

For the Hollandaise sauce
2 egg yolks
120g unsalted butter (melted)
1 tablespoon lemon juice
Freshly ground black pepper

2 – 4 eggs
4 - 6 slices cooked ham

For the buns
Mix all the dry ingredients together in a mixing bowl, add the warm water, mixing with your hands to form a soft dough. Turn out onto a floured work surface and knead, dusting with more flour if sticky, continue to knead until soft and springy. Divide into 2 pieces, work each with your hand to form buns, a medium-sized roll with a flattened top and bottom. Heat the pan on low heat, add a very small amount of oil, carefully put in the buns, put the lid on and cook on low heat for about 7 minutes each side. They should be very slightly golden on each surface, hollow to tap, and well risen. Take out, set aside.

Fry the eggs gently in a little oil. Cut the buns in half, put on serving plate, place a slice of ham on each half, top with the eggs.

For the Hollandaise sauce
Whisk the egg yolks, lemon juice and pepper in a sauce pan on medium heat as the mixture thickens (30 seconds or so) pour in the butter, whisking hard - the mixture will become very smooth and silky, take off the heat and pour directly over the cooked eggs. Season and serve immediately with hot coffee.

Makes: 2 – 4 portions

Blinis
with asparagus

Blinis with asparagus

A delicate light lunch or supper dish

For the blinis
130g plain white flour
1/2 teaspoon baking soda
a large egg
100ml milk

120g green asparagus
Sprigs of dill
Black sea salt flakes and freshly ground black pepper

Oil for frying

Utensils: bowl, frying pan, spatula, small pan, slotted spoon, iced water, kitchen paper.
Equipment: hob

Bring to the boil a small pan of water.
Remove the asparagus bases, cut the asparagus in half.
Boil for 1 minute, take out and plunge into iced water.
Drain and dab dry with kitchen paper.

For the blinis
Combine flour and baking soda together in a large bowl.
Make a well in the centre, add the egg and milk, combine until you have a thick smooth batter.
Finely slice some of the cooked asparagus and add to the batter, season with salt and pepper.
Heat a little oil in a heavy bottomed frying pan until hot, (wipe with kitchen paper to remove excess oil).
Spoon the batter (about a tablespoon) onto the hot pan, leave space between each spoonful and cook the blinis for 1 minute each side (flip over carefully with a spatula) - put on the serving plates.
Arrange the asparagus tips on the top, serve with crème fraiche and fresh dill.

Makes: 2 - 4 portions

Quiche

Quiche

A meal in itself at any time, eat fresh on the day with a crisp green salad. It keeps well in the fridge, serve cold with chutney.

Utensils: tart tin 20-22cm diameter x 4cm deep, mixing bowls, knife and chopping board, grater
Equipment: oven

For the filling
200g cheese (medium – mild hard)
200ml double cream
100g spring onions
100g red pepper (flesh weight)
50g celery
25g fresh parsley
4 whole eggs
Salt and freshly ground black pepper

For the tart base
180g plain white flour
110ml olive oil
½ teaspoon salt
30ml water

Extra olive oil

For the tart base
Pre-heat the oven to 190c. Grease the tart tin with a drizzle of oil.
Combine the flour and salt in a large bowl. Add the oil and rub it in with your fingers, add the water and bring together to form a soft dough. Press into the oiled tin, covering the base and sides with an even thickness. Make sure the pastry dough comes up to the top of the tin, the pastry should be thin and even. Set aside in the fridge.

For the filling
Grate the cheese. Peel and finely slice the onion. Finely slice the pepper. Finely chop the celery and the parsley.
In a large bowl whisk the eggs together, add the cream, season well. Add all the rest of the ingredients, mix thoroughly and pour into the uncooked pastry case.
Bake in a hot oven, centre to bottom shelf for 40 minutes until lightly golden and just firm to touch. Remove and leave to cool in tin for at least 30 minutes before serving.

Makes: 1 medium sized tart – 6 portions

French onion soup

French onion soup

This is a quick version but still takes a while to prepare - it freezes well so you could make a batch and take it out when you need it.

Utensils: chopping board and knife, grater, mandolin (if you have one)
Equipment: hob and heavy based saucepan

For the beef stock	For the onion soup
500g beef marrow bones	*400g mild sweet white onions*
40g onion	*2 large cloves garlic*
30g celery	*1 tablespoon fresh parsley*
3 cloves garlic	*1 bay leaf*
2 bay leaves	*2 tablespoons extra virgin olive oil*
1 small bunch fresh parsley	*700ml beef stock*
1 sprig thyme	*100ml white wine*
2 teaspoons black peppercorns	
1.5 litres water	*Croutons and grated cheese*

For the stock
Peel the onion and garlic, roughly chop. Roughly chop the celery and parsley. Put all the ingredients into a large pan with the water, bring to the boil, turn down the heat and simmer gently for 1 hour. Strain and use as directed.

For the soup
Finely slice the onions (a mandolin is useful otherwise get them as thin as you can). Peel and finely grate the garlic. Finely chop the parsley.
Heat the oil in a heavy based pan, add the onions and bay leaf, cook on medium-high heat until soft and lightly golden (5 - 8 minutes) stir from time to time, do not allow to blacken.
Add the beef stock (about 1 litre), garlic and parsley, bring to the boil, turn down the heat, season well, cover and simmer for 15 minutes.
Serve in individual bowls with croutons (cubes of fried bread) and finish with a little grated cheese on top.

Makes: 2 – 4 servings

Cooking note: for this quick recipe, it is very important to use sweet mild onions - Spanish variety.

Simple pan fried fish

Simple pan fried fish

There's nothing like simple grilled or pan-fried fish, a little olive oil and lemon - the taste of the sea.

Utensils: chopping board and knife, frying pan, spatula or tongs, kitchen paper
Equipment: hob

200g cod fillet
Bunch fresh parsley finely chopped
2 cloves garlic
1 Lemon
Sea salt flakes and freshly ground pepper
2 tablespoons extra olive oil

Peel the garlic and finely slice.
Pat the fish dry with kitchen paper and season well.
Heat the oil in a frying pan on medium heat, add the fillets and fry for 2 minutes each side, toss in the garlic and herbs, cover, turn off the heat and leave to sit for 2 minutes. Serve with a wedge of lemon (and bread to mop up the juices or a pile of chips).

Spare ribs
spring rolls

Spare ribs and spring rolls

Loads of effort, maximum enjoyment

Utensils: large bowl, large shallow dish for marinating the ribs, oven tray and kitchen foil.
Equipment: oven

1000g pork spare ribs
2 large onions
2 tablespoons sesame oil

For the marinade
1 tablespoon soft brown sugar
3 tablespoons soy sauce
2 tablespoon Worcestershire sauce
4 tablespoons ketchup
3 cloves garlic - grated
20g fresh ginger root - grated
1 teaspoon ground ginger
1 teaspoon Chinese five spice (or allspice)
1 teaspoon paprika or pimenton
Pinch of freshly ground pepper

Combine all the ingredients for the marinade in a large bowl.
Put the ribs into a large shallow dish and cover with the marinade. Use your hands to rub into the meat all over.
Cover tightly with cling foil and leave to marinate for 24 hours.

Pre-heat the oven to 240 degrees C.
Line the oven tray with kitchen foil.
Peel the onions and thickly slice, lay on top of the foil, drizzle with sesame oil.
Place the marinated ribs on top and pour over any remaining marinade.
Bake in the hot oven on the top middle shelf for 15 minutes.
After 15 minutes, turn the ribs over and cook for a further 15 minutes.
Take the ribs out, cover tightly with kitchen foil, return to the oven but turn the oven off. Leave the ribs to sit in the oven for a further 30 minutes.
Take out and serve.

The ribs can be served hot or cold and they are easy to warm through in the foil. You can make them as part of an Oriental style supper, serving with spring rolls and rice. The onions in the base of the tray are delicious served as a side dish. If there is a lot of juice left on the tray, cook in a pan with the onions for a few minutes to reduce into a thick sauce.

Makes: 4 - 8 portions

Cooking note: If you like the ribs more sticky, don't cover them with foil but instead cook them on the highest shelf in the oven and cook for 20 minutes each side until crispy – you'll have much less sauce left over after cooking but the ribs will be crispier. If you don't have Chinese five spice you can grind up cinnamon, anise, peppercorns and fennel seeds.

Spring Rolls

Utensils: chopping board and knife, peeler, grater, large pan, spatula
Equipment: hob

175g cabbage
125g spring onions
75g mushrooms
40g coriander
40g fresh ginger root
2 tablespoons extra virgin olive oil
Salt and pepper
3 sheets of filo pastry (30x40cm, cut in half)

Oil for shallow frying

Finely shred the cabbage and the onions.
Clean and slice the mushrooms.
Peel and finely grate the ginger.
Finely chop the coriander, including the stalks.
Heat 2 tablespoons of oil in a large pan until hot and smoking. Add all the ingredients and rapidly stir fry on the high heat, constantly moving all ingredients around in the pan for 1 minute. Counting sixty seconds whilst stirring is often easiest. Don't overcook. Season and turn out into a bowl and leave to cool.
Lay out the filo pastry rectangle sheets and lay a small strip of the cabbage mixture in the middle.
Moisten the edges of the pastry with a drizzle of olive oil, fold over the ends and then roll up the roll as tightly as possible. This should make 6 cigar shaped rolls. Work on one roll at a time and line them up on a plate ready for frying.
Heat up the oil in a shallow pan until hot and cook each roll for about 1 minute until lightly golden.

Makes: 6 rolls

See page 74 for image.

Bakewell tart

Bakewell tart

This is best freshly baked – it will disappear at all times of the day, going well at coffee or tea, dessert or late night snack.

Utensils: tart tin 20 – 22cm diameter 4 cm deep, two large mixing bowls, grater, whisk, spatula
Equipment: oven, food processor

For the tart base
200g plain white flour
40g caster sugar
125g butter (unsalted, softened)
Pinch of salt
25ml warm water
Extra butter to grease the tart tin.

For the filling
150g ground almonds
150g butter (unsalted, softened)
150g caster sugar
3 large eggs
1 lemon (zest only)
7 tablespoons raspberry jam

50ml amaretto liqueur

Pre-heat the oven to 190 degrees C.
Grease the tart tin thoroughly with a little butter.
Combine the flour, caster sugar and salt in a large bowl. Rub in the softened butter with your fingertips until you have formed loose crumbs.
Add the warm water and bring together to form a soft dough.
Press into the buttered tin, covering the base and sides with an even thickness – make sure the pastry dough comes up a little beyond the top of the tin. Set aside in the fridge.

Finely grate the lemon zest. Combine the sugar and butter in a large bowl, whisk in the eggs, fold in the almonds and lemon zest.
Spread the raspberry jam on the base of the uncooked tart, spoon the almond filling over, bake on low shelf for about 40 minutes until just firm (the outer edges will feel firmer than the middle).
Take out of the oven, pour the amaretto over the top and leave to cool.
Dust with icing sugar; serve with or without crème Anglaise (custard) - see page 83 for recipe.

Makes: 1 tart, 6 portions

Apple & almond Strudel

Apple and almond strudel

Thin layers of pastry encompassing softly spiced apple and almond paste

Utensils: large bowls, saucepans, conical sieve, whisk, oven tray, greaseproof paper, pastry brush
Equipment: oven, food processor – stick blender

4 large apples (800g weighed whole)
150g whole almonds (skins on)
70g sugar
60g sultanas
60g unsalted butter
100ml double cream
3 eggs
4 - 5 sheets of filo pastry 30 x 40cm
1 tablespoon lemon Juice
1 teaspoon cinnamon

Pre-heat the oven to 200 degrees C.
Line the baking tray with greaseproof paper.
Grind the almonds in the processor with 1 teaspoon sugar until fine.
Peel the apples, discard the core and cut into thin slices.
Place the apple slices and lemon juice into a small saucepan on low heat, cook gently for 5 minutes until soft. Drain off the excess juice, add the cinnamon and sultanas. Mix until combined and set aside to cool.

In another bowl beat together 2 of the eggs, the cream and sugar. Cook over low heat, whisking all the time to thicken (do not burn). Take off the heat and use the stick blender to churn the mix, tip into a large bowl. Add the ground almonds and mix into a thick paste.

Beat up the remaining egg in a small bowl.
Melt the butter in a small pan.

To assemble the strudel

Start by laying one sheet of filo pastry down on the baking tray.
Brush generously with butter and then place another sheet of filo on top, starting half way across.
You'll end up with two sheets overlapping in the middle.
Take another sheet and cut in half and lay across that middle section. Brush generously with butter every time you layer or fold over the pastry.

Spoon out the almond mixture in a long sausage like strip across the reinforced middle section of your pastry.

Place the apples on top. It will look like too much but pile them all on.

Brush the ends of the filo with butter and fold both over the apple.
Fold over one middle side and then the other, as tight as you can.
Brush the whole strudel with butter and place a new sheet of pastry around it, brush again and place another. You may not be able to roll the strudel but just place the sheet of pastry on top and tuck the ends underneath. You can also patch small cracks with strips of pastry but don't worry too much, the pastry will crack a bit in the oven anyway. Brush with the beaten egg to seal it.
Bake in the hot oven, middle shelf for 15 - 20 minutes until golden.
Take out and leave to cool slightly.
It can be eaten hot or cold, dusted with icing sugar, served with cream, ice cream or custard.

Makes: 4 – 6 portions

Cooking note: filo can dry out quickly so have a damp tea towel handy to cover as necessary. The apple mixture should be cool and well drained before you start to construct the strudel.

Custard (crème anglais)

250ml double cream
100g caster sugar
2 large eggs
5 drops natural vanilla extract or 1 vanilla pod (softened if necessary in a little hot water, split it down the middle with a shrp knife and scrape out the seeds – add these to the cooked custard)

Utensils: pan, whisk, mixing bowl, serving jug
Equipment: hob

Crack the eggs into the mixing bowl, add the sugar and cream, whisk until smooth. Transfer to a pan and cook on low heat, whisking constantly until it thickens (make sure it doesn't stick to the pan or burn). As soon as it has thickened, remove from the heat, whisk in the vanilla and pour into the serving jug.
Serve warm or cold.

Makes: 2 – 4 servings

Cooking note: This is a rich custard, whisking makes it smooth and light, when chilled it is thick. For a runnier custard, you can use half milk, half cream. For a thick set custard add one more egg yolk.

Chocolate tart

Chocolate tart

A moist rich tart particularly good after dinner in small quantities

Utensils: small pan, whisk, mixing bowls, spatula, tart tin 20 - 22cm diameter x 5cm deep
Equipment: Oven, hob, food processor - whisk (optional)

For the pastry
225g flour
50g caster sugar
150g softened unsalted butter
50ml warm water
Pinch of salt
Butter for greasing

For the filling
100g dark chocolate 70% cocoa
170ml double cream
50g organic dark cocoa
170g caster sugar (100g plus 70g)
5 egg yolks
2 egg whites

Pre-heat the oven to 220 degrees C.
To prepare the tart base, grease the tart tin thoroughly.
Combine the flour, sugar and salt in a large bowl, add the butter, rub in with your fingers. Add the water and bring together to form a soft dough. Press into the tin, making sure the pastry is an even thickness all over the base and up the sides – allow the pastry to come up a little beyond the top of the sides. Set aside in the fridge.

For the filling
Break up the chocolate into small pieces, combine with the cream in a small pan and melt on a low heat.
When thoroughly melted, whisk in 100g sugar.
Remove from heat and transfer to large mixing bowl, whisk in the egg yolks and cocoa powder, leave to sit.
In another bowl, whisk the egg whites until stiff, add the remaining sugar (70g) slowly, whisking all the time until stiff and glossy.
Carefully fold the egg whites into the chocolate mix.
Pour into the prepared tart base and bake in the hot oven, bottom self for 20 - 25 minutes.
Take out of oven and leave to cool in the tin (the tart will rise and sink a little).

Makes: 1 tart, serving approximately 6 portions

Bread

Bread

Of all the things that go into making a place a home there's nothing quite like the aroma of freshly baked bread.

Utensils: large mixing bowl, oven tray lightly oiled, knife
Equipment: oven

500g unbleached white flour, wholemeal or a mix
20g easy action dried yeast
1 tablespoon caster sugar
1 teaspoon salt
1 tablespoon extra virgin olive oil
Warm water 200 – 300ml

Pre-heat the oven to 240 degrees C.
Put the flour, sugar and salt into a large bowl, mix a little, add the yeast and mix thoroughly using your hands.
Make a well in the centre of the flour, add the oil and about 200ml warm water.
Bring the dough together, drawing the flour from around the edges of the bowl.
Add more water as necessary to bring the dough to a soft 'loose' consistency - do not make it too firm.
Dust the work surface with flour and knead the dough, pulling towards you and pushing it back – use the sides and base of palms. Knead for about 3 minutes.
Cut the dough, shape into two loaves and dust with flour and slash the tops lightly with a knife.
Place on an oiled oven tray and leave in a warm place until doubled in size.
Bake in the hot oven, middle shelf for about 20 minutes.
When done, they should be light golden and will make a hollow sound when tapped.
Leave to cool on wire rack before cutting.

Makes: 2 loaves

Scones for tea

Scones for tea

Classic tea time treat, best eaten straight from the oven so make more than you think you will need!

Utensils: small knife, pastry cutter 3 - 4cm diameter, fork, mixing spoon, large bowl, baking parchment, fine sieve, ruler
Equipment: oven

200g plain white flour
50g butter (softened)
30g caster sugar
2 teaspoons baking powder
1/2 teaspoon salt
90ml milk
1 large egg
Flour for dusting

Pre-heat the oven to 220 degrees C. Line the oven tray with baking parchment.
Sieve the flour and baking powder into a large bowl. Mix in the sugar.
Rub in the softened butter with your fingertips.
Pour in the milk and beaten egg, bring together with your hands to form a soft dough.
Dust your hands with a little more flour, turn out onto a floured surface and knead a little, very lightly.
Roll or press into a flat shape about 3cm thick, dust with flour.
Cut out rounds using a pastry cutter (if you don't have a cutter, cut round a small coffee cup or glass with a sharp knife).
Place the rounds onto the parchment lined oven tray. Re-form the dough using all the cuttings until you have used it up. Bake in the hot oven for 12 minutes until just coloured.
Eat warm with strawberry jam or cold with clotted cream and fresh strawberries.

Makes: about 6 large scones

Orange and almond cakes

Orange and almond cakes

Textured, light cakes with subtle flavours that combine really well.

Utensils: mixing bowl, grater, sieve, silicone or paper cup cake cases
Equipment: oven, food processor

100g melted butter
150g sugar
300g white flour
1 teaspoon baking powder
3 sweet oranges
150g almonds (with skins)
4 eggs

Preheat the oven to 190 degrees C.
Sieve the flour and baking powder into a large mixing bowl.
Finely zest the oranges and then juice.
Grind up the almonds with a spoonful of sugar in the processor until fine.
Separate the eggs.
Whisk the egg whites until stiff peaks, add in the sugar little by little and continue beating until glossy.
Mix all the ingredients together, starting by adding the ground almonds to the flour, then add in the egg yolks, butter, orange zest and juice. Stir all together thoroughly.
Carefully fold in the stiff egg whites.
Fill paper or silicone cupcake cases with the mixture.
Bake in the hot oven, centre shelf for about 17 - 20 minutes, until risen and golden on top.

Makes: about 24 small cakes

Butter shortbread

Butter shortbread

A traditional shortbread is made in one piece and is scored ready to be broken into rectangular fingers. The top has small indentations which help to the sprinkled sugar to stay on.

Utensils: mixing bowl, knife, baking parchment, rolling pin (optional)
Equipment: oven

200g plain flour
50g caster sugar
140g unsalted butter (very soft and cut into small pieces)
Pinch of salt
Extra caster sugar for sprinkling over the tops

Pre-heat the oven to 160 degrees C. Line the baking tray with parchment.
Mix the flour, salt and sugar together in a large mixing bowl.
Rub in the butter with your thumbs and forefingers to form fine crumbs, then pull together to make one lump of dough (it should just hold, do not knead).
Transfer the dough straight to the lined baking tray and pat down flat using your hands. You are aiming to make a rectangular flat block with straight edges all round, (you can do this by tapping the outside edges with the back of a large knife) the thickness should be a minimum of 1cm. Press into shape with the palms of your hands or use a rolling pin very lightly if you wish.
Score lines with a sharp knife, pressing all the way down to create rectangular biscuits. When you have all your biscuits scored, prick the tops and dust with caster sugar.
Bake in the oven for 25 - 30 minutes - they want to be a pale colour, so keep an eye on them towards the end of cooking. When done, leave to cool completely on the tray - they will firm up enough to handle, and to break cleanly apart. Perfect with a cup of tea.

Makes: about 10 biscuits

Cooking note: the trick to making these melt-in-the-mouth biscuits is to bring the mix together with a very light touch. You can cut the biscuits into shapes using a pastry cutter if you prefer.

Walnut and coffee cake

Walnut and coffee cake

A birthday or anytime cake with two old fashioned flavours that combine really well.

Utensils: sieve, mixing bowls, whisk, cake tin 22 - 24 cm diameter, baking parchment, spatula
Equipment: oven, food processor

400g plain white flour
1 teaspoon baking powder
180g softened butter
240g caster sugar
4 large eggs
60ml very strong espresso coffee
125g walnuts
50g walnuts for decoration

For the frosting
20ml espresso coffee
50g icing sugar
80g softened butter

2 egg whites
50g icing sugar

Pre-heat the oven to 200 degrees C. Line the cake tin with baking parchment.
Sieve the flour and baking powder into a large bowl.
Chop the walnuts roughly in the processor.
Separate the eggs. Cream the butter with 180g of sugar in a large mixing bowl, whisk in the egg yolks then add to the sieved flour.
Add the walnuts and coffee, combine thoroughly.
Whisk the egg whites to soft peak, add the remaining sugar 60g and whilst to thick glossy peaks.
Fold into the cake batter. Spoon into a prepared tin and bake middle shelf for 30 minutes.
When ready the cake should be golden and lightly firm to touch - leave to cool in the tin. To serve, cover with the frosting or simply dust with icing sugar.

Makes: 1 cake, about 8 portions

For the frosting.
In a bowl whip the butter with a spoon, add the icing sugar and the coffee and continue to whip until you have a soft paste - set aside.
Whisk the egg whites to form stiff peaks, fold in the icing sugar and whisk until glossy.
Fold the egg whites into the coffee butter and refrigerate for 20 minutes. After cooling you should have a frosting that you can apply with a palette knife to the cake.

Ice creams

Ice creams

Making ice cream is easy and you don't need any special equipment. Once you have the basic mix you can add flavours - the addition of sweetened condensed milk helps the scoop-ability.

Utensils: bowls, whisk, large saucepan
Equipment: hob

500ml double cream
3 eggs
2 tablespoons sweetened condensed milk
120g caster sugar
2 vanilla pods

Put the cream and sugar into a large mixing bowl, whisk together. Crack open the eggs and whisk into the mix. Put the mix into a large pan on low heat and cook very gently, whisking continuously until thick and frothy. Remove from the heat and transfer back into the big bowl. Whisk in the sweetened condensed milk.
At this point you can add a flavouring such as vanilla or you could divide the mixture to make different flavourings from one batch.

To make vanilla ice cream add 2 vanilla pods. These need to be softened in a little warm water first. Split them in half lengthways with a sharp knife and scrape out the seeds, whisk into the cooked mix. Pour into an airtight container and freeze for at least 8 hours.

To make chocolate ice cream, add 80g organic cocoa to the cooked mix and whisk in thoroughly.

To make strawberry or mango ice cream, add 200 - 300g pureed fresh fruit to the cooled, cooked mix and whisk in thoroughly.

Makes: 1 tub ice cream, about 10 portions

Cooking note: You can 'churn' the ice cream half way through the freezing process to help the scoop-ability. Working quickly, put the part frozen ice cream into the food processor and blend rapidly, spoon back into the airtight container and put back into the freezer

PICNIC

Muffins 100 - 101

Chicken satay 102 - 105

Fishcakes 106 - 109

Beignets 110 - 111

Carpet picnic 112 - 115

Spanish breakfast 116 - 117

Mini pizzas 118 - 119

Chicken wraps 120 - 122

Smörgåsbord 122 - 123

Samosas 124 - 127

Muffins

Muffins

These muffins all have a similar batter base with the addition of different vegetables and seasonings, the variations are endless.

Utensils: sieve, mixing bowls, spatula, whisk, grater, muffin tins or silicone moulds
Equipment: oven

For carrot and cumin muffins
250g white flour
1 teaspoon baking powder
2 eggs
230ml milk
120g carrots
80g mild hard cheese
70g onion
1 teaspoon cumin seeds
1 teaspoon turmeric
Pinch of salt and pepper

To make courgette muffins: *substitute 200g courgettes (finely grated) for the carrots, omit the cumin and turmeric.*

To make chorizo muffins: *substitute 150g chorizo (finely diced) for the carrots, add 1 tablespoon parsley (finely chopped) and 1 teaspoon pimenton, increase milk to 250ml.*

Pre-heat the oven to 200 degrees C.
Finely grate the cheese. Peel and finely slice the onion. Peel and finely grate the carrots. In large bowl sieve the flour, baking powder and a pinch of salt, add the cumin and turmeric. In another bowl, whisk together the milk and eggs. Add the milk mixture to the flour and then add in the onion, carrots, cheese and pinch of pepper. Mix until combined but don't over mix, you want the ingredients to just come together. The mixture should be a good dropping consistently and should fall easily off a spoon. Add a splash of extra milk if it feels a little stiff.
Spoon the mixture into lined muffin tins. Bake in the hot oven, middle shelf for 30 minutes until risen and golden.

Makes: 12 - 14 muffins

Chicken satay

Chicken Satay

A long prep so do the day before – a sort of bench picnic overlooking the view, served in containers with a fork for the Thai cucumber salad.

Utensils: chopping board and knife, prep bowls, dish for marinade, small pan, spoon, grater, 12 long wooden skewers
Equipment: Hob, oven, food processor

To make the chilli syrup
For both the marinade and the peanut sauce, chilli syrup is used here. It's a great addition to the store cupboard and very simple to make - here's the recipe to make a bottle full as it lasts a long time!

150ml water
150g caster sugar
10 small chillies

Trim and roughly chop the chillies, combine with the sugar and water in a small pan, cook on low heat until the sugar has dissolved and a light syrup has formed. Cool and bottle.

For the marinade
1 large stick lemon grass
3 cloves garlic
20g fresh ginger root
30ml light sesame oil
40ml soy sauce
40ml chilli syrup
1 teaspoon turmeric
1 teaspoon ground coriander
1 teaspoon ground cumin
1 large scallion (white part)

2 chicken breasts

To make the marinade
Peel and roughly chop the lemon grass, garlic and ginger.
Combine all the ingredients together and blend in the food processor to make a paste, transfer to a large container (dish or bowl).
Cut the chicken breasts into long thin strips. Put them into the marinade, making sure they are thoroughly covered. Cover with kitchen film and refrigerate for a minimum of 4 hours.

Note: for a vegetarian version you could use cubed tofu and pre-cooked vegetables which need to be par-baked ie, not fully cooked. Red onion segments, large cubes of sweet potato, cubed squash and cubed aubergine, lightly sautéed work well.

For the peanut sauce
100g unsalted peanuts
150ml coconut milk
1 teaspoon tamarind paste
2 tablespoon fresh lime juice
1 tablespoon light sesame oil
1 tablespoon chilli syrup
1 teaspoon soy sauce
2 cloves garlic

Peel and finely grate the garlic.
Combine all the ingredients together and blend in the food processor, leave the peanuts slightly coarse so that the sauce has some texture. Taste and adjust to your liking – it should have a balance between sweet and sour, salty and spicy.

To cook
Pre-heat the oven / grill to 240 degrees C. Line the oven tray with foil.
Soak the wooden skewers in water for 5 minutes.
Thread the marinated chicken strips onto the skewers (leave a good length free to handle).
Place the skewers on the foil and cook under the grill for 5 minutes each side.

Serve with the peanut sauce, Thai cucumber salad and fragrant rice

Thai cucumber salad

This is a really nice refreshing salad that must be made on the day

200g cucumber (skin on – green skinned Dutch or English variety)
50g mild white onion
20g fresh ginger root
2 tablespoon chilli syrup
2 table spoon rice vinegar (or apple cider vinegar will do)
1 large red chilli

Trim and de-seed the chilli, discard the seeds, cut the flesh into long, very thin strips. Finely slice the cucumber (as fine as you can) use a mandolin if you have one, season with salt. Peel and finely slice the onion, again as thin as you can get it.
Peel and finely grate the ginger root (discard the fibrous end bit).
Combine the chilli syrup, vinegar and ginger in a large bowl. Add the cucumber slices, white onion and chili. Serve immediately with or with out fresh coriander leaves.

Makes: 4 portions

Thai cucumber salad

Fish cakes

Fishcakes

This recipe is very hands on and takes some time but the results are worth it. It has three stages starting with cooking the fish and the potato, then constructing the fishcakes and covering them in breadcrumbs and finally frying in oil ready for eating.

Utensils: chopping board and knife, frying pan, medium sized pan, various bowls, large spoon and potato masher, grater, fork
Equipment: hob, food processor

200g salmon fillet
200g potatoes
30g mild white onion
15g fresh coriander
½ lemon (zest and juice)
3 cm fresh ginger root
1 tablespoon tomato ketchup (natural quality brand)

1 large egg
1 slice white bread (cut into pieces)
2 tablespoons white flour
30g polenta

Oil for frying

Prepare the salmon
Remove any bones and skin, cut the fillet up into cubes. You can easily steam the pieces in a microwave for a couple of minutes or steam them in a frying pan on the hob. To do this put a small amount of water in the bottom of the pan on low heat, drop in the cubes, cover and poach, this takes about 3 – 5 minutes. You will need to check that the water does not boil dry, add a little more as necessary, not too much as to make the salmon watery. The salmon will go lighter in colour as it cooks. When cooked remove the pieces with a spoon and set aside in a large bowl.

To cook the potatoes
Put a medium sized pan filled with water on to boil.
Peel and cut the potatoes into evenly sized cubes, add to the water and boil for about 7 minutes – until the potato pieces are soft but still intact (test this with a sharp knife, it should pass through easily). Transfer the potatoes to a bowl and mash until smooth.

To construct the fishcakes

Peel and finely chop the onion.
Finely chop the coriander.
Zest the lemon (fine grate) and juice.
Peel and grate the ginger root.

Combine the fish, potato, onion, coriander, ginger, lemon and tomato ketchup in the large bowl. Mix thoroughly using your hands to form a firm evenly textured paste. Divide into four if you want large fishcakes, or divide into 12 for small. Mould into patties, flatten slightly.

Crack open the egg into a small bowl and mix with a fork.
To make the breadcrumbs put the polenta, flour and slice of bread into the processor and churn until you have even fine crumbs. Turn out into a bowl.

Using your hands, dip each fishcake into the egg then into the crumbs, making sure that every surface is well covered. Set aside the prepared fish cakes on a plate ready to fry. At this point they can be refrigerated until you are ready to cook.

When ready to serve, deep fry the fish cakes in hot oil until golden brown. Serve with a wedge of lemon or lime and tomato relish.

Makes: 4 – 12 fishcakes depending on size

Tomato Relish

Two variations for a fresh, slightly sweet and spicy relish.

Utensils: chopping board and knife, grater, medium sized pan, prep bowls
Equipment: hob, food processor - blending stick

500g tomatoes
150g onion
2 garlic cloves
1 length of fresh ginger root– about 6cm
50g caster sugar
30ml white wine vinegar
Pinch of salt

Peel and finely chop the onion.
Trim and finely dice the tomatoes.
Peel the ginger and garlic and finely grate.
Put the tomatoes, onion, garlic and ginger into the pan and place onto medium heat. Cook with a lid on for 5 minutes, stirring once or twice.
Add the vinegar, sugar and salt, turn the heat down low. Let the relish cook for about 25 minutes, until the liquid has well reduced. Then use a blender stick to churn the mixture up a bit. Pour into a sterilised jar.

This second variation is more spicy with a sweet sour undertone and an extra hot kick.

Add to the recipe above
1 tablespoon cumin seeds
1 tablespoon tamarind paste
1 tablspoon lime juice
1 teaspoon ground cinnamon
1 teaspoon fresh chilli chopped or dried chilli flakes

Both relishes store well for about 1 month in the fridge.

Cauliflower Beignets

Cauliflower beignets (batter fritters)

This is a lovely light fritter recipe and the cauliflower can easily be replaced by other vegetables. You can even fry spoonfuls of the batter on their own and toss in cinnamon and sugar for a sweet treat.

Utensils: chopping board and knife, large bowl, large pan, iced water, spider spatula, kitchen paper
Equipment: hob

250g white flour
200ml warm water
140ml beer
Generous pinch of salt
2 tablespoons extra virgin olive oil
3 egg whites
500g cauliflower, cut into small florets
About 1 litre oil for deep frying

Sieve the flour into a large bowl and make a well in the centre.
Add the salt, water, beer and oil, whisk together, drawing the flour in from the sides. Leave the mixture to sit for a minimum of half an hour.

Bring a pan of water to the boil, add the cauliflower florets and boil for 5 minutes. Drain immediately, submerge into iced water to prevent the cauliflower from cooking further. Drain again, set aside.

Whisk the eggs whites until stiff peaks and then gently fold them into the batter. Heat the oil in a large pan. When hot, dip the florets into the batter and then drop them carefully a few at a time into the oil - don't over crowd the pan. Fry them for about 1 minute 30 seconds, turning them over half way. When ready they should be a light golden colour. Remove the fritters from the oil, drain on kitchen paper. Keep frying in small batches until you've used up all your batter and cauliflower.
Sprinkle the beignets with salt and serve immediately. They are especially good with tomato relish - see page 109 for recipe.

Makes: about 12 fritters

Carpet picnic

Carpet picnic

A gathering of deli-foods, a bottle of the best you can afford and your best-loved movie. Some ideas: humous, smoked salmon, tzatziki, prosciutto di Parma or Serrano ham, sliced cheeses, fresh tomato salad, marinated olives, lettuces, fresh bread, pickles and chutney, something sweet – almond macaroons.

Here are four recipes to get you started.

Humous

A creamy dip of pureed chickpeas.

Utensils: chopping board and knife, spoon, sieve
Equipment: food processor

400g cooked chickpeas (natural jarred variety)
4 teaspoons tahini paste (sesame seed paste)
2 large cloves garlic
3 tablespoons extra virgin olive oil
2 teaspoons lemon juice
Sea salt and freshly ground black pepper

Drain the chickpeas and rinse in water, drain and put into the food processor. Peel and roughly chop the garlic.
Combine all the ingredients (except the olive oil) in the processor and churn until smooth, add the olive oil and churn again. Season sparingly with salt (or not at all) and generously with pepper.

Makes: 4 – 6 portions or 2 if you love it!

Tzatziki

A refreshing cucumber dip.

Utensils: chopping board and knife, mixing bowl

200ml thick Greek yoghurt
100g cucumber
15g fresh dill
2 cloves garlic
1 tablespoon lemon juice
1 teaspoon sugar syrup
Pinch of salt and freshly ground pepper

Combine the lemon juice and sugar syrup in a bowl.
Finely chop the dill, stir into the lemon and sugar mix.
Peel and very finely dice the cucumber and the garlic, add to the mix.
Stir in the yoghurt and season lightly.

Makes: 2 – 4 portions

Marinated olives

Utensils: grater, bowl, spoon, storage jar

200g large green olives with pips
2 cloves garlic
1 tablespoon cumin seeds
1 teaspoon dried chilli
1 teaspoon sugar syrup
100ml extra virgin olive oil

Peel and finely grate the garlic. Combine all the ingredients in a small bowl. Drain the olives, add to the bowl, mix thoroughly, bottle and leave to marinade for at least 24 hours.

Makes: 1 jar marinated olives

Almond macaroons

Utensils: spoon, oven tray and baking parchment
Equipment: oven, food processor

150g almonds in their skins
150g icing sugar
4 egg whites
Extra almonds for decoration

Pre-heat the oven to 150 degrees C. Line the oven tray with baking parchment.
Grind the almonds in the processor until very fine.
Whisk the egg whites until stiff add the sugar slowly, fold in the almonds. Spoon the mixture in small mounds onto the tray, leaving space between, press an almond lightly into each one and bake for 30 minutes, middle shelf, cool oven.
Leave to cool, store in airtight container.

Makes: 10 – 20 depending on size

Spanish breakfast

Spanish Breakfast

This is one to take into the garden on a warm sunny morning for a good breakfast/ brunch. Spaniards get up early in the heat and stop around 10.30 for breakfast: strong dark coffee, toasted bread, olive oil and juicy tomatoes, washed down with a slug of something strong and sweet.

There are no quantities listed below because you can throw together as much as you need and there's barely need for instructions.

Reading from the image left to right, front to back

Fresh spicy chorizo - sliced thinly and gently warmed for a few minutes on a low heat.

Salted almonds - toasted in a little oil in a frying pan for about 5 minutes on low heat, tossed in fine salt.

Brown country bread – cut into slices.

Marinated olives – green olives, cumin seed, crushed garlic and pimenton.

Tomatoes – fresh ripe vine tomatoes, finely diced, sprinkled with a pinch of sea salt.

Best quality extra virgin olive oil to drizzle.

Mini pizza rounds

Mini Pizza Rounds

These make excellent picnic or party food - prepare the toppings first.

Utensils: chopping board and knife, prep bowls, mixing bowls, grater, baking tray, baking parchment,
Equipment: oven

Topping A
50 g feta cheese (finely diced)
20g sundried tomatoes (pre-soak and roughly chop)
1 - 2 cloves of garlic (peeled and finely sliced)
Freshly ground black pepper

Topping B
80g mild hard cheese (finely grated)
50g mild white onion (peeled and finely sliced)
1 tablespoon dried oregano

400g white flour
1 tablespoon easy action dried yeast
1 tablespoon olive oil
1 teaspoon caster sugar
250ml warm water
Pinch of salt
Extra virgin olive oil for drizzling

Preheat the oven to 240 degrees C, line the oven tray with parchment.
Mix the flour, sugar, salt and yeast in a large bowl. Add in the water and oil, mix together. Turn the dough out onto a floured work surface, if the dough is too sticky, sprinkle with more flour and knead for about 3 minutes until it is smooth and springy.
Divide the dough into 20 small pieces and form each piece into a ball by rolling the dough between the palms of your hands. Then flatten the circle out to create a mini pizza base. Place the bases onto the tray, distribute topping A over one half and topping B on the other.
Drizzle with a little olive oil and bake in a hot oven, bottom shelf for 8-10 minutes, until the cheese is melted and the bottoms golden.

Makes: 20 mini pizzas

Chicken wraps

Chicken wraps - lemon chicken, blackened pepper and vine tomato

Pan-fried flat bread is quick and easy to make and perfect for these wraps. Prepare all the fillings first and fry the bread last.

Utensils: chopping boards and knife, prep bowls, spatula, grater, medium-sized heavy bottomed frying pan, saucepan, kitchen foil or lid
Equipment: hob

400g chicken breasts
2 tablespoons cornflour
2 tablespoons extra virgin olive oil
1 small lemon
Sea salt and freshly ground black pepper
4 large green peppers
1 tablespoon extra-virgin olive oil

400g vine tomatoes
40g spring onions
2 little gem lettuces
Dressing or mayonnaise of your choice (see p.41 for recipes)
Cocktail sticks

For the flat bread wraps
300g plain white flour
1 tablespoon easy action dry yeast
½ teaspoon salt
½ teaspoon caster sugar
1 tablespoon extra-virgin olive oil
100ml warm water
Extra flour for dusting

Cut the chicken breasts into thin strips, season well and dust all over with cornflour, sauté in hot olive oil for 1 minute each side to seal, add 2 tablespoons water, immediately cover, turn down the heat and cook gently for 5 minutes.
Zest and juice the lemon, add to the cooked chicken, keep covered and set aside.

Heat the oil in a medium sized pan, add the peppers (keep whole) and sauté on high heat both sides for 2- 3 minutes until you have good blackened marks. Add a splash of water and cover immediately, turn down the heat and cook for 5 minutes to soften. Leave to cool a little, then remove stalk and seeds, set aside.

Trim the tomatoes, lettuce and scallion, finely slice, set aside.

In a large bowl, combine the flour, salt, sugar and yeast, mix thoroughly, add the olive oil and water, bring together to form a soft dough. Turn out onto a floured work surface and knead for a few minutes until you have a soft springy dough. Divide and shape into four balls. Flatten each ball into a thin disc about 20cm diameter.
Heat the frying pan (without oil) until hot, cook the flat breads dry for 1-2 minutes each side, they should be lightly golden.

Lay out the cooked wraps and fill, starting with the lettuce, strips of tomato, onion, cooked peppers and chicken strips. Drizzle with dressing or mayonnaise, wrap up and secure with a cocktail stick.

Makes: 4 generous wraps

Smörgåsbord

Smörgåsbord is a buffet spread of a variety of food typically from the Scandinavian region. It's fun to make and you can include whatever you fancy, here are some ideas as a starting point.

Reading from the image front to back.

Thinly sliced rye bread, half a gherkin pickle, thinly sliced white onion, ½ a boiled egg, a pinch of black pepper and chives

Small seared salmon pieces, ½ raspberry and a couple of capers.

Sesame seed bread, sour cream, fish eggs and a sprig of dill.

Little gem lettuce leaf, langoustine and a little dill mustard.

Smörgåsbord

Samosas

Samosas

Tasty, spicy go anywhere snack.

Utensils: chopping board and knife, medium sized pan and spatula, small bowl and fork, grater, pastry brush
Equipment: oven, hob

1 medium sized carrot
1 small leek
1 small courgette
1 green pepper
1 small apple
2cm length fresh ginger root
1 large clove garlic
1 teaspoon ground turmeric (or curry spice mix)
Handful fresh coriander
2 tablespoons extra virgin olive oil
Sea salt
Freshly ground black pepper

6 filo pastry sheets – 20x30cm
1 egg
Extra virgin olive oil for drizzling

Pre-heat the oven to 220 degrees C.
Peel the carrots, cut into fine strips.
Trim the leek, remove the outer layer, cut into thin strips.
Top and tail the courgette, cut in half, slice lengthways into strips and then cut each strip into fine sticks.
Trim the pepper, remove seeds and cut into fine strips.
Peel the apple, discard the core and finely dice the flesh.
Peel the ginger and the garlic, finely grate.
Roughly chop the coriander.

Heat the oil in the pan, toss in all the vegetables (except the ginger, garlic and coriander), sauté for 3 minutes on medium heat, stirring all the time and then add in the garlic and ginger, cook for 1 more minute and then remove from the heat, add the turmeric and coriander, season with salt and pepper and set aside to cool.

Crack the egg into a small bowl, whisk with a fork.

To construct the samosas, make one at a time as the pastry can dry out quickly. It's also important that the filling is cool.

Take out a sheet of pastry and lay it flat on the work surface, drizzle with olive oil. Cut a 10cm strip from one side of the piece and place it in the middle to make a second layer this will reinforce the samosa bases. On top of this distribute 1/6 of the cooked mixture (you can divide ahead of time to ensure even distribution between the samosas.)

Brush all-round the edge of the pastry with egg. Fold two opposite sides over to cover the mixture. Brush the top with more egg, fold over the remaining sides to form a square. (Or you can make any shape, triangle or cigar for example).

Drizzle with olive oil and place on a lined baking tray. Repeat and construct all six pastries. Try to work quickly to avoid the pastry breaking.
Bake in a hot oven for about 15 minutes until golden.
Serve hot or cold.

Makes: 6 small samosas

Cucumber dip

A refreshing dip that goes particularly well with the spiced samosas.

Utensils: chopping board and knife, mixing bowl

200ml thick Greek yoghurt
100g cucumber
50g mild sweet white onion
30g fresh mint leaves
1 tablespoon lemon juice
1 tablespoon sugar syrup
Pinch of salt and freshly ground pepper

Combine the lemon juice and sugar syrup in a bowl.
Very finely chop the mint, stir into the lemon and sugar mix.
Peel and very finely dice the cucumber and the onion, add to the mix.
Stir in the yoghurt and season lightly.

Makes: 2 – 4 portions

Sugar syrup

A light syrup that can be flavoured with anything from chilli and mint to lemon and redcurrants - a useful addition for any store cupboard.

Utensils: small pan and whisk
Equipment: hob

200g caster sugar
200ml water

Combine the sugar and water in a small pan, place over low heat and stir until the sugar has melted and a light syrup has formed. Bottle and store.

ENTERTAINING

Prawn timbale with dill 130 - 131

Red onion tart 132 - 133

Chicken terrine 134 - 137

Fricasee of monkfish 138 - 141

Beef Wellington 142 - 145

Dressed seabass 146 - 147

Pavlova 148 - 149

Raspberry soufflé 150 - 151

Lemon tart 152 - 153

Prawn timbale with dill

Prawn timbale with dill

An easy to prepare supper dish, make in advance and chill.

Utensils: chopping board and knife, small pans, conical sieve, 2 small moulds (about 120ml), palette knife, kitchen film
Equipment: hob, food processor

100g fresh cooked large prawns
100g salmon fillet (skin removed)
40g sweet white onion
20g butter (unsalted)
1 tablespoon double cream
1 teaspoon fresh dill (finely chopped)
Freshly ground pepper
75ml water (5 tablespoons)
1 sheet gelatin (1g - cut up into small pieces)
2 tablespoons lemon juice

To prepare the moulds, line with kitchen film, leaving a generous overlap.
Peel the prawns and extract the waste vein (run a sharp knife along the top of their spines and pull out the vein), rinse in cold water, dab dry, cover with kitchen film and set aside in the fridge.

Put the 75ml water into a small pan, bring to the boil. Lower the salmon fillet in and poach gently for about 2 minutes. Take out the fillet, check for bones, put the cooked fish into the food processor.
Peel and finely chop the onion, sauté in butter (using the same small pan) on low heat for 3 minutes until translucent. Add to the cooked fish in the processor. Add the cream and chopped dill, churn until smooth.
Put the lemon juice and gelatin into a small pan on low heat until dissolved, add to the fish mix in the processor and churn thoroughly, turn out into a bowl.
Slice the prawns into 2 or 3 pieces, add to the fish, season with pepper and spoon the mixture into the prepared moulds, use a palette knife to smooth the top surface flat, cover with kitchen film and refrigerate for at least 2 hours.
To serve, turn out the moulds, remove the cling film and garnish with a fresh sprig of dill or chives.

Makes: 2 portions (large starter size)

Cooking note: you can also use agar agar instead of gelatine to lightly set this - use 2 teaspoons in hot lemon juice, heat to a light paste.

Red onion tart
rocket & balsamic dressing

Red onion tart, rocket and balsamic dressing

Crumbly, light pastry, sweet soft onions, a hint of balsamic vinegar and the peppery rocket leaf.

Utensils: chopping board and knife, large mixing bowl, medium sized pan, 4 tart tins about 9cm diameter with removable bases
Equipment: oven, hob

600g red onions
100ml extra virgin olive oil

Peel and finely slice the onions.
Cook the onion slices in the olive oil in a medium sized pan on high heat for 3 minutes until coloured, stir constantly. Turn down the heat and leave to cook slowly for a further 30 minutes until caramelized. Stir from time to time. Once cooked, set aside.

For the dressing	For the tart bases
1 tablespoon balsamic vinegar	*180g white flour*
1 clove garlic (finely grated)	*75ml extra virgin olive oil*
1 teaspoon smooth mustard	*1/2 teaspoon of salt*
1 teaspoon mild runny honey	*1 tablespoon warm water*
2 tablespoons extra virgin olive oil	
Pinch of salt and pepper	

Pre-heat oven to 240 degrees C.
To make the tart bases, put the flour in a large bowl, add all the other ingredients and bring together with your hands. Do not over work. Divide the pastry into 4 balls and press each into oiled tins. Bake the bases in a hot oven for approximately 8 - 10 minutes until lightly golden. Set aside to cool slightly in their tins.
Fill the tarts with the cooked onions and then remove them carefully from the tins, place directly onto the serving plate.

To make the dressing, whisk together all the ingredients until thoroughly combined.

Pile a few rocket leaves on top of each tart, spoon over a little of the dressing, season and serve immediately.

Makes: 4 small individual tarts

Chicken terrine
with bacon & apricots

Chicken terrine with bacon and apricots

An impressive feat to make and to serve. It's not made in a traditional terrine mould and baked in the oven but is poached in water rather like a ballotine. It needs to be made well in advance and keeps well in the fridge for up to five days.

Utensils: chopping board and knife, prep bowls, large pan with lid or kitchen foil, cling film, rubber bands,
Equipment: hob, food processor,

500g chicken breasts (approximately 2 breasts)
100g onion
80g sultanas
2 large garlic cloves
1 tablespoon dried oregano
1 tablespoon fresh parsley
1/2 teaspoon salt
1/2 teaspoon freshly ground pepper

Cut the chicken breast up into small pieces.
Peel and roughly chop the onion and garlic. Finely chop the parsley.
Put all the ingredients into the food processor and churn until it's a well combined textured paste. Tip out into a bowl and set aside.

100g dried apricots
50g bacon
Freshly ground pepper

Finely slice the apricots and the bacon. Put in the processor, season well with pepper and churn lightly until it's a well combined textured paste. Tip out into a bowl and set aside.

300g chicken breast (approximately 1 large breast)
150g thinly sliced bacon (approximately 12 slices)

Cut the chicken breast into four long strips lengthways.
Cut off any rind from the bacon.

To construct:
Lay out 8 large pieces of cling film, over-lapping at least two layers to form a sheet about 25cm wide x 30cm long.
Lay the bacon slices on top running them vertically, overlapping top to bottom and side to side.

Spread the chicken mixture over the centre, leaving about 4cm top and bottom clear – that is, leaving some of the bacon uncovered.

Place the chicken breast strips in two horizontal lines along the centre, leaving a small gap between them.

Place the apricot mixture (in a line) in the gap between the two rows of chicken strips.

Roll up the whole thing to form a long sausage. Use the cling film to help roll and over-lap the free pieces of bacon as you finish the sausage. Twist the cling film at each end to loosely secure.

Lay out some more cling film in layers, place your sausage on top and roll up in more film, rolling tighter. Secure each end with a rubber band and fix tightly.

Poach the terrine in a large pan of boiling water for 45 minutes
When done, carefully remove. Leave to cool for a minute or two then carefully unwrap and snip the ends off (both the cling film and rubber band) over a big bowl so that you can collect the juices. Then rewrap the terrine in lots of cling film, pressing and pulling tightly all the time to "press" the terrine. When firmly wrapped put 2 more rubber bands round each end to secure and refrigerate for at least 6 hours (overnight is best).

To serve, cut with a sharp knife into thick slices. It's best to cut straight through the cling film, then to carefully remove the film from each individual slice afterwards. Serve with toast, chutney and a drizzle of nut oil.

Makes: 8 portions

Cooking note: the bacon must be thinly sliced but can be smoked if you like.

Tomato and apple chutney

Utensils: chopping board and knife, large pan, stirring spoon, jars for bottling
Equipment: hob

400g tomato
250g onions
250g white sugar
200g apples
50g sultanas
250ml white wine vinegar
2 teaspoons ground ginger
1 teaspoon ground cinnamon

Trim the tomatoes and finely dice.
Peel and finely chop the onions.
Peel the apple, remove the core and finely dice.
Put all the ingredients into a pan on medium heat and bring to the boil, stir well, turn down to simmer and cook on low heat for 30 – 40 minutes, until the chutney is thick with very little excess liquid. As it nears the end of cooking, stir well to avoid burning. Remove from the heat, bottle into clean jars and cap tightly.
This will keep well in the fridge for weeks but you can also sterilize the jars if you want to keep them in your store cupboard. To do this lightly scrunch up a large sheet of tin foil and place it in the bottom of a medium sized pan, place the jars on top (lids very tightly on), fill the pan with hot water to cover the jars and put on high heat to boil. Boil for 10 minutes to sterilize. Leave to cool a little before removing the jars from the water.

Makes: approximately 5 x 200ml jars

Fricasee of monkfish
with spring vegetables

Fricassee of monkfish with spring vegetables

Easy to please all guests with this dish, monkfish is a meaty fish, boneless and easy to cook. There's a fair amount of prep but most can be done in advance.

Utensils: chopping board and knife, medium sized pan, colander, potato masher, peeler, large frying pan with lid or kitchen foil, spatula, bowl of iced water, prep bowls
Equipment: hob

500g monkfish tails weight without bone (bone saved for stock)

For the seasonal vegetables
100g carrots
100g leeks
100g courgettes
80g broccoli spears
80g fennel
80g baby closed cap mushrooms
80g green asparagus
A few sprigs of fresh fennel or dill

For the fricassee stock
Monkfish tail bone
1 large onion
2 cloves garlic
2 sticks celery
1 handful fresh parsley
1 handful fresh dill
2 bay leaves
1 dessertspoon whole black peppercorns
Small pinch of saffron threads
100ml white wine
50g unsalted butter
100ml double cream
Sea salt and freshly ground black pepper

To make the fricassee stock
Peel and roughly chop the onion and garlic.
Roughly chop the celery, parsley and dill.
Put the monkfish tail bones in a large pan with 1 litre of water, bring to the boil.
Add the onion, garlic, celery, bay leaves, parsley and dill, simmer for 30 minutes.
Add the wine, simmer for a further 15 minutes.
Strain and put back into the pan, add the saffron, butter and cream. Simmer gently to reduce a little, season to taste. The stock is now ready to reheat just before serving.

For the chive mash
500g potatoes
20g unsalted butter
1 tablespoon finely chopped chives
Pinch sea salt

To make the chive mash
Peel and cut the potatoes into quarters (all roughly the same size).
Boil in a generous amount of boiling water for 20 – 30 minutes until soft.
Drain thoroughly, transfer to a large bowl, add the butter and a little salt, mash until smooth. Add the chopped chives, cover and set aside.

To prepare the vegetables
Peel and cut the carrots lengthways into 4, cut into short even sticks, blanch in boiling water for 1 minute, then immediately plunge into iced water, drain and set aside.
Trim the leeks, remove the outer layer(s) cut diagonally into short lengths, blanch in boiling water for 1 minute, then plunge into iced water, drain and set aside.
Trim the broccoli, cut into small spears, blanch in boiling water for 1 minute, plunge into iced water, drain and set aside.
Trim the asparagus, cut into short lengths, blanch for 30 seconds, plunge into iced water, drain and set aside.
Trim the fennel, cut in half and finely slice. Cook in a little olive oil on low heat for 2 minutes, set aside.
Trim the courgettes, cut lengthways into 4, cut into short even sticks. Cook in a little olive oil on low heat for 1 minute, set aside.
Clean and trim the mushrooms, cook in a little olive oil on low heat for 1 minute, set aside.

Toss all the prepared cooked vegetables together in a bowl. Season, drizzle with extra virgin olive oil and transfer to a pan ready to warm through, after you have cooked the fish.

When ready to serve, season the frying pan with a minute amount of oil. Use kitchen paper to rub evenly over the base – heat on high to very hot.
Sear the monkfish (whole tails) on high heat for 1 minute (don't move them), then turn over and sear the other sides for 1 minute (again don't move them).
Remove from the heat and immediately add 1 tablespoon water, and immediately cover. Leave covered, set aside to rest for 5 minutes (this time allows the fish to steam to just done).

Meanwhile gently warm the vegetables on low heat.
Reheat the mashed potatoes (best to microwave these if you have one) otherwise heat and stir very gently on the hob.
Reheat the stock gently on the hob.
Cut the fish into generous slices.
Place a spoon of mash in the middle of the serving plates. Scatter the vegetables around, pour over the stock, arrange the fish slices on top, garnish with small sprigs of dill. Serve immediately.

Makes: 4 portions

Cooking note: best to warm the plates in the oven before serving.

Beef Wellington
with beetroot and mash

Beef Wellington

This classic dinner party piece is a 'hands on' dish from start to finish, you can prep some of the dish in advance up to the stage of chilling the beef and pastry but for the final construction and cooking the chef needs to be in the kitchen right up to serving to table. The preparation of the dish is in four parts: the beef is seared, then surrounded by a layer of chopped mushrooms (duxelles), then wrapped in a pancake (to absorb juices) - this is chilled then wrapped up in pastry and cooked in the oven. The making of the dish starts with the pancakes.

Utensils: chopping board and knife, prep bowls, large mixing bowl, rolling pin, whisk, large heavy based frying pan, spatula, large plate, kitchen film, baking parchment, pastry brush, fork, roasting tongs, large roasting fork
Equipment: oven, hob, food processor (optional)

To make the pancake
80g plain flour
2 large eggs
150ml whole milk
Oil for frying the pancakes

Crack open the eggs and whisk lightly in a large bowl, add the milk and flour, continue to whisk until you have formed a smooth batter. Put the frying pan on high heat, add a little oil, turn the pan so that the entire base is covered. The aim is to make large, thin pancakes. Pour in a little of the batter, turning the pan as you do to help spread the batter over its entire base. Cook for around 30 seconds, then turn the pancake over with a spatula, cook for another 30 seconds, tip the pancake out onto a large plate. They should be lightly golden both sides, repeat until all the batter has been used. Set the pancakes aside.

It can take some experience to make the perfect pancake especially for this recipe where they must be thin and as large as you can get them, so keep making until you achieve this - you can make the batter looser or heavier by adding a little more milk or flour respectively.

For the duxelles
200g mushrooms
2 shallots
2 cloves garlic
10g fresh parsley
1 tablespoon extra virgin olive oil
20g unsalted butter
Salt and freshly ground black pepper

Peel and finely chop the shallots, garlic and mushrooms. Finely chop the parsley, you can use the food processor if you like but don't over chop to become mushy. Put the oil and butter in a pan over medium heat and sauté all the prepared ingredients for about 5 minutes until they are cooked and most of the liquid has been absorbed, season, tip out and set aside.

500g fillet beef (whole cylindrical piece – look for a piece about 8cm diameter)
1 tablespoon extra virgin olive oil
20g unsalted butter
Salt and freshly ground black pepper

1 tablespoon Dijon mustard

Season the beef fillet. Put a large heavy based frying pan onto high heat, add a little olive oil and sear the beef on all sides for 2 – 3 minutes, sear the ends as well using the tongs or roasting fork, remove from heat, set aside to rest.

Lay out 4 – 6 large layers of cling film out on the work surface making sure that they are over lapping – you need a large final layered piece about 50 x 50 cm. Lay your pancakes out on top of the cling film, over lapping slightly. Spread the duxelles over the top. Place the seared beef fillet in the middle, smear the beef lightly all over with the mustard and wrap the entire lot up, fold the ends of the pancake in to surround the beef, wrap tightly in the kitchen film, folding the ends over as you roll. Wrap in more cling film if necessary to make a firm fat sausage. Chill in the fridge for about 1 hour.

For the pastry
180g plain white flour
110ml olive oil
½ teaspoon salt
30ml water

Pre-heat the oven to 240 degrees C.
Combine the flour and salt in a large bowl, add the oil and rub it in with your fingers, add the water and bring together to form a soft dough. Lay out a large sheet of baking parchment about 50cm wide x 30cm long. Put the pastry on top and press out flat and even with your hands. Lay another piece of parchment on top and use the rolling pin to roll out a thin layer of pastry between the two sheets of parchment. The size needs to be about 40cm x 30cm, the thickness of the pastry should be about 2mm. Chill (leave flat) in the fridge for a minimum of 20 minutes.

1 large egg (cracked into a small bowl and forked to mix)

Final construction and cooking
Remove the pastry and beef from the fridge. Place the pastry (with its two layers of parchment still on) directly onto the oven tray. Carefully take the top layer of parchment off the pastry.
Remove the film from the pancaked wrapped beef and place the beef centrally on top of the pastry. Roll up, tucking the ends in as you go. Pinch the overlaps of pastry together with your finger tip, pressing together to seal. Glaze all over with egg wash, make two slits on the top with a sharp knife (this will allow the steam to vent during cooking) and put in the hot oven, middle shelf for about 30 minutes until the pastry is golden. Take out and set aside to rest for at least 5 minutes before carving and serving.

Lots of dishes accompany this well but unless you have more hands in the kitchen perhaps creamed potatoes (see page 140) and wilted greens are some of the easiest to serve, these you can prep in advance - French fries and broccoli would be alternatives but both require last minute cooking.

Makes: Beef Wellington to serve 4 people

Dressed seabass
with avocado & kiwi salad

Dressed seabass with avocado and kiwi salad

A delicate, elegant supper or light lunch dish, challenging to prepare but worth it.

Utensils: chopping board and knife, large frying pan, kitchen foil, long spatula, fine sieve, small pan, small whisk
Equipment: hob

1 whole seabass (gutted and scaled about 500g)	For the garnish
500g sweet Spanish white onions	4 quail eggs
4 bay leaves (fresh if possible)	3 black olives (pitted)
10 whole peppercorns	Thin slices of cucumber
1 small bunch of dill	(peeled)
1 large bunch parsley	Fresh rosemary sprigs
200ml white wine	1 teaspoon powdered
300ml water	agar agar

For the salad
1 kiwi (peeled and sliced)
1 avocado (peeled and sliced)
a few green grapes (peeled and halved)
Extra virgin olive oil, squeeze of lemon

Peel and finely slice the onions, spread them over the base of the frying pan. Place the peppercorns, bay leaves, dill and parsley on top. Lay the whole fish on top (if your fish is too long for your pan you can, if necessary cut the head and tail off at this point). Pour in the water and wine, cover tightly with a lid or foil. Place on medium heat, bring to a simmer and poach the fish covered in the liquor for 20 minutes. Leave to cool in the pan (covered) for about 30 minutes. Carefully lift the fish out of the pan using a long spatula, remove the head and tail using a sharp knife, peel off the the skin and the joining piece in the centre back. Put the clean, cooked fish onto your serving plate.

Cook the quail eggs for 5 minutes in boiling water (adding a little vinegar helps to loosen the shell). Peel and cut in half, slice a small piece off each so that they sit flat. Strain the fish cooking liquor and re heat 200ml. Add the agar agar, mix well using a small whisk until thickened. Pour a layer all over the dressed fish, put the fish in the freezer for 2 minutes, then place the cucumber slices on top of the fish, followed by the quail eggs, place a slice of olive in the centre of each one, position the rosemary sprigs either side. Pour over another layer of jelly and put in the fridge for 5 minutes until lightly set, repeat with a final layer of jelly (reheat lightly if necessary). Leave to set in the fridge. Neaten up the excess jelly around the base of the fish and serve garnished with sliced kiwi, grapes and avocado, drizzled with a little olive oil and lemon juice.

Makes: 1 whole fish to serve 2 people

Pavlova
with summer fruits

Pavlova with summer fruits

Probably best not to even suggest where this dessert originated from but suffice to say that it is a light meringue nest, crisp on the outside and soft in the middle, filled with vanilla cream and soft summer fruits.

Utensils: large mixing bowl and whisk or electric whisk, spoon, piping bag, greaseproof paper or silicone sheet
Equipment: oven, food processor - whisk (optional)

4 large egg whites
200g caster sugar
2 teaspoons cornflour
1 teaspoon apple cider vinegar

200ml double cream
1 tablespoon icing sugar
1/2 teaspoon vanilla extract
500g fresh soft fruit such as strawberries, raspberries and redcurrants

Pre-heat the oven to 90 degrees C. Double line the oven tray with greaseproof paper or silicone.
Whisk the egg whites until stiff, add the sugar slowly and whisk vigorously for a few minutes until you have stiff glossy peaks. Gently whisk in the cornflour and vinegar.
Spoon or pipe out the meringue into small individual 'nests', build up the edges higher than the centre, leave plenty of space between each one as they expand a little during cooking.
Bake in a cool oven for 1 hour 30 minutes or so until the meringues are crisp.
Prepare your choice of soft fruits, slice or finely dice, the image shows wild strawberries, raspberries, blueberries and lavender flowers.
Whisk the cream until stiff, fold in the vanilla and icing sugar.
To serve, lift the nests carefully off the baking tray, fill the centres with cream and pile the prepared fruit on top.
Serve immediately.

Makes: about 8 nests

Cooking note: If you don't have a piping bag, fill a small plastic bag with the mixture and snip a small corner off at the bottom.

Raspberry soufflé

Raspberry soufflé

A delicate soufflé as light as a feather.

Utensils: ramekins or small oven proof dishes (this recipe fills approximately 2 at 125ml capacity or 4 at 50ml) conical sieve and spoon, small pan and potato masher, bowls
Equipment: food processor or whisk and bowl, oven and hob

150g fresh raspberries
30g caster sugar
1 tablespoon lemon juice
2 teaspoons cornflour
2 teaspoons water
2 egg whites plus 30g caster sugar
A little melted butter and sugar for the ramekins
Icing sugar for dusting

Pre-heat the oven to 180 degrees C.
Prepare the ramekins, brush with melted butter then dust with sugar.
Put the raspberries, lemon juice and sugar into a small pan, use the potato masher to macerate - mash into the sugar. Put onto low heat and warm through to dissolve sugar (1 - 2 minutes).
Pass through a conical sieve, collect the puree in a bowl.
Mix the cornflour with the water and add to the raspberry puree. Set aside to cool.
Whisk the egg whites to soft peak, add the sugar slowly, whisk until glossy. Fold carefully into the cool puree until well mixed.
Spoon into the prepared ramekins (ideally the mixture should come to 1 cm below the rim). Using your thumb, run round the top of the mixture along the inside of the top surface, this helps the soufflé for maximum rise.

Bake in the pre-heated oven for 12 minutes.

Remove and serve immediately – you have about 3 - 5 minutes before they start to deflate so be quick!

Makes: 2 – 4 soufflés

Lemon tart

Lemon tart

This is a really lemony tart! The recipe uses 8 egg yolks which you need to separate from the whites, you are therefore left with 8 egg whites which you could use to make the pavlova on page 149.

Utensils: tart tin 20 – 22cm diameter 4 cm deep, two large mixing bowls, fine grater or zester, whisk
Equipment: oven, stick blender

For the tart base	For the filling
200g plain white flour	350g mascarpone
40g caster sugar	220g caster sugar
125g butter (unsalted and softened)	8 egg yolks
Pinch salt	4 lemons
25ml warm water	
A little extra butter for greasing the tart tin	

Pre-heat the oven to 200 degrees C. Grease the tart tin. Combine the flour, caster sugar and salt in a large bowl. Rub in the softened butter with your fingertips until you form loose crumbs. Add the warm water and bring together to form a soft dough. Press into the tin, covering the base and sides with an even thickness – make sure the pastry dough comes up a little, beyond the top of the tin. Set aside in the fridge.

Lightly zest all four lemons then juice (you need 150ml).
Combine the juice and zest and churn with a stick blender. (this helps to extract the zestiest, most lemony flavour).
Whisk the egg yolks, caster sugar and mascarpone together until very smooth. Add the churned juice and zest, mix thoroughly.
Pour into the prepared pastry case. Carefully put into the hot oven, lower shelf, and bake for 50 minutes.
After 50 minutes, it will be golden, wobbly but firm enough to lightly touch, it will have risen slightly above the pastry case and may sink a little.
Take out and leave to cool in the tin. Then refrigerate to set (leave in the tin) allow at least 6 hours. Serve on its own or with red fruits.

Makes: 1 tart, 6 portions

INDEX

INDEX

A
Almond
bakewell tart 79
muesli bar 15
orange cake 91
Apple
and almond strudel 81
Asparagus
with blinis 67
Aubergine
lamb tagine 25
moussaka 37
stuffed with spinach, lentils and sweet potatoes 40
Avocado
and kiwi salad 147
mozzarella and fresh figs 55

B
Bacon
and coriander salad 57
Basil
fresh figs and mozarella 55
Beans
aduki, meatless balls 28
Beef
wellington, en croute 143
Biscuits
butter shortbread 93
Blinis
with green asparagus 67
Bread
buns 65
mini pizza rounds 119
olive oil 87
pan baked wraps 121

C
Cabbage
spring rolls 77
Cake
orange and almond 91
walnut and coffee 95
Caper
smorgasbord 122
Cannelloni
stuffed spinach and mushrooms 33
Carrot
and cumin muffins 101
Cauliflower
beignets 111
Caviar
smorgasbord 122
Cheese
cannelloni 33
feta, greek salad 51
quiche 69
mozzarella, fig and avocado 55

Chicken
asian with cashew nuts 23
lemon wraps 121
terrine 135
satay 103
sesame, glazed with tamarind 31
Chickpea
humous 113
Chicory
orange and langoustine 59
Chilli
syrup 103
Chocolate
ice cream 97
mexican tart 85
Chorizo
new potato, rocket and peppers 21
muffins 101
spanish breakfast 117
Chutney
tomato and apple 137
Cinnamon
lamb tagine 25
Coconut
big breakfast bowl 17
Coffee
and walnut cake 95
Courgette
muffins 101
Couscous
fragrant orange 23
Cucumber
and mint dip 127
thai salad 105
tzatziki 114
Cumin
and carrot muffins 101
bean balls 28
Custard
creme anglais 83

D
Dates
tagine, lamb 25
Dill
prawn timbale 131

E
Eggs
benedict 65

F
Feta
greek salad 51
mini pizza rounds 119
Figs
mozzarella and basil 55
Fish
dressed seabass 147
fishcakes 107
fricasee of monkfish 139
Pan fried 73

G
Garlic
ravioli, manchego, serrano ham 46
Gherkin
smorgasbord 122
Ginger
fishcakes 107
samoosas 125
thai cucumber salad 105
tomato relish 109
Granola
big breakfast bowl 17

H
Ham
serrano, ravioli 46
Hazelnut
big bowl breakfast, granola 17
Honey
muesli bar 15

I
Ice cream
from scratch 97

J
Jelly
dressed seabass 147

K
Ketchup
spicy tomato relish 109

L
Lamb
moussaka 37
tagine 25
Langoustines
chicory and orange salad 59
timbale (mousse) with dill 131
Lemon
tart 153
Lentils
aubergine stuffed 40
vegetarian sausages 43
Lime
bean balls with spicy tomato sauce 28

M
Macaroon
almond 115
Mascarpone
lemon tart 153
Melon
hawaiian salad 53
Meringue
pavlova with summer fruits 149
Mozzarella
figs, avocado and basil 55
Muffin
carrot, chorizo, courgette 101
Muesli
bar 15
big breakfast bowl 17
Mushroom
cannelloni 33
stuffed 19

N
Noodles
to accomany asian chicken 23

O
Oats
muesli bar 15
big bowl breakfast 17
Olives
greek salad 51
marinated 114
spanish breakfast 117
Olive oil
bread 87
spanish breakfast 117
Onion
caramelized red onion tart
french onion soup 71
Orange
and almond cake 91

P
Pancake
blini 67
cannelloni 33
Paw paw
hawaiian salad 53
Pasta
ravioli, serrano, manchego 46
Peaches
big bowl breakfast 17
Peanut
satay sauce 104
Peppers
chorizo, new potatoes and rocket 21
Pimenton
spiced sesame chicken 31
Pork
spare ribs 75

Potato
andalucian salad 61
chive mash 140
chorizo and rocket 21
fishcakes 107
Prawn
timbale with dill 131
chicory and orange salad 59
Prunes
muesli bar 15

Q
Quiche
cheese and onion 69

R
Raspberry
soufflé 151
smorgasbord 122
Rice
basmati with asian chicken 23
to accompany spare ribs 76
Rocket
chorizo and potatoes 21

S
Salad
andalucian 61
bacon and coriander 57
greek 51
hawaiian 53
langostine, chicory and orange 59
Salmon
prawn timbale with dill 131
smorgasbord 122
Samosas
from scratch 125
Sausage
vegetarian 45
Scones
traditional 89
Seabass
dressed 147
Sesame
spiced chicken with tamarind glaze 31
Shortbread
traditional 93
Smorgasbord
ideas for 122
Soufflé
raspberry 151
Soup
french onion 71
Spinach
cannelloni with mushrooms 33
Strawberry
pavlova 149
Ice cream 97

Strudel
apple and almond 81
Syrup
chilli 103
sugar 127
Sweet potato
aubergine stuffed 40

T
Tagine
lamb 25
Tart
quiche 69
red onion 133
Tamarind
glazed, sesame chicken 31
Tomato
and apple chutney 137
relish 109
sauce 29
spanish breakfast 117
Terrine
chicken 135

U

V
Vanilla
ice cream 97
Vegetable
crisps 44
Vinaigrette
basic 41
herb 41
orange 59

W
Walnut
and coffee cake 95

X

Y
Yoghurt
cucumber and mint dip 127
tzatziki 114

Z
Zucchini
muffins 101

Kitchen store cupboard

Rice (short - risotto and long grain - basmati), wild rice
Dried pasta (spaghetti, other)

Couscous (easy cook), polenta, raw oats,

Jarred quick cook stand-by: chickpeas and white beans (100% natural brand)

Dried pulses: white beans, mung beans, black eyes beans, lentils (puy), chickpeas

Tinned: sweetcorn, pineapple, olives, gherkins, capers

Flours: plain white flour, wholemeal brown flour, corn flour

Baking: baking powder, baking soda, easy-action yeast, gelatine sheets, agar agar powder, liquid glucose, vanilla pods and extract (100% natural)

Cocoa powder and espresso coffee

Sugars: white caster sugar, soft brown sugar, icing sugar, molasses and golden syrup
Mild honey and sweetened condensed milk

Oils: extra virgin olive oil, light sesame oil, walnut or hazelnut oil (small quantity), oil for deep frying

Vinegars: balsamic, white wine and apple cider vinegar

Sauces: tomato ketchup (homemade or 100% natural brand), brown sauce (such as HP brand), Worcestershire, horseradish, wasabi and soy
Smooth and grain mustard
Chilli syrup (homemade or 100% natural brand)
Sugar syrup (homemade)
Chutney (homemade or 100% natural brand)
Red currant jelly
Red fruit jam, apricot jam and orange marmalade

Dried Herbs: rosemary, bay leaves, oregano, thyme

Nuts and seeds: whole almonds, hazelnuts, walnuts, white sesame, poppy, pumpkin and sunflower seeds

Dried fruit: sultanas, apricots, prunes

Spices: cinnamon, cloves, star anise, pimenton, curry mix, turmeric, cumin seeds, dried chillies, black pepper corns, fine sea salt and sea salt flakes

Fridge: milk, butter, cheese, yoghurt, crème fraiche, double cream, eggs, mascarpone
Soft fruits, salad, fresh vegetables and herbs
Frozen: petits pois, stand-by spinach

Potatoes, onions and garlic, apples, oranges and lemons